First World War
and Army of Occupation
War Diary
France, Belgium and Germany

2 CAVALRY DIVISION
Divisional Troops
Royal Army Service Corps
2 Cavalry Division Ammunition Park (56 Company A.S.C.)
20 August 1914 - 12 June 1916

WO95/1128/3

The Naval & Military Press Ltd
www.nmarchive.com
Published in association with The National Archives

Published by

The Naval & Military Press Ltd

Unit 10 Ridgewood Industrial Park,

Uckfield, East Sussex,

TN22 5QE England

Tel: +44 (0) 1825 749494

www.naval-military-press.com

www.nmarchive.com

This diary has been reprinted in facsimile from the original. Any imperfections are inevitably reproduced and the quality may fall short of modern type and cartographic standards.

© Crown Copyright
Images reproduced by permission of The National Archives, London, England, 2015.

Contents

Document type	Place/Title	Date From	Date To
Heading	WO95/1128/3		
Heading	2nd Cav Div troops 2nd Cav Div Ammn Park (56 Coy ASC) 1914 Aug-1917 Sep		
Heading	2nd Cavalry Div Ammn. Park Vol. I 16-31.8.14		
War Diary		20/08/1914	31/08/1914
Heading	2nd Cavy: Div: Ammn Park Vol 5.10.-31.12.14		
War Diary		05/10/1914	31/12/1914
Heading	2nd Cavy: Ammn Park. Vol III. 1-31-1-15		
War Diary		01/01/1915	31/01/1915
Heading	2nd Cavy Div Ammn Park. Vol IV 1-28-2-15		
War Diary		01/02/1915	28/02/1915
Heading	2nd Cav: Div Ammn Park. Vol V 1-31.3.15		
Miscellaneous	Herewith my diary for the month of March 1915.		
War Diary		01/03/1915	31/03/1915
Heading	2nd Cav: Divl: Ammn Park. Vol VI 1-30.4.15		
War Diary		01/04/1915	30/04/1915
Heading	2nd Cavy: Divl: Ammn Park. Vol VII May 1915		
Miscellaneous	Herewith diary for may 2 Cav. Div. Gun Park.		
War Diary		01/05/1915	31/05/1915
Heading	2nd Cav Division. 2nd Cavy: Divl: Gun: Park Vol VIII 1-30.6.15		
War Diary		01/06/1915	30/06/1915
Heading	2nd Cavalry Division. 2nd Cav Divl Gunn Park. Vol X 1-31-7-15		
War Diary		01/07/1915	31/07/1915
Heading	2nd Cavy Division 2nd Cav: Divl: Gunn Park. Vol XI 1-31.8.15.		
War Diary		02/08/1915	31/08/1915
War Diary		01/08/1915	01/08/1915
Heading	2nd Cavalry Division. 2nd Cavy: Divl: Gunn Park Vol XII Sept. 15		
War Diary		01/09/1915	30/09/1915
Heading	2nd Cavalry Division. 2nd Cavy. Divl Gun Park Vol XIII Oct. 15		
War Diary		01/10/1915	31/10/1915
Heading	2nd Cavalry Division. 2nd Cavalry Division 2/Cav. Gun Pk Nov. Vol XIV		
War Diary		01/11/1915	30/11/1915
Heading	War Diary of 2nd Cavalry Division Ammunition Park From 1st 12/15 to 31st 12/15 Vol XV.		
War Diary	Avroult	01/12/1915	31/12/1915
Heading	War Diary 2nd Cavalry Division Ammunition Park From 1 1/16 To 31 1/16 Volume XVI		
War Diary	Tailly (Near Lillers)	01/01/1916	01/01/1916
War Diary	Park Situated on His Lillers-Bethune Road 3/4 of a Mile East of Cools Roads between Bas-Rieux (N.E) and Haut-Rieux (S.W.)	01/01/1916	01/01/1916
War Diary	Tailly (Near Lillers)	02/01/1916	04/01/1916
War Diary	Tailly	05/01/1916	31/01/1916

Heading	War Diary of 2nd Cav. Div. Ammtn Park. From 1st February to 29th February 1916 Vol XIV		
War Diary	Tailly	01/02/1916	21/02/1916
War Diary	Avroult	22/02/1916	29/02/1916
Heading	War Diary of 2nd Cav. Div. Ammtn Park. From 1st February To 29 February 1916		
Heading	War Diary of 2nd Cavalry Division Ammtn Park. From 1st to 31st March 1916 Vol XVIII		
War Diary	Avroult	01/03/1916	31/03/1916
Heading	War Diary of 2nd Cavalry Division Ammtn Park From 1st to April 1916 Vol XIX		
War Diary	Avroult	01/04/1916	30/04/1916
Heading	War Diary of 2nd Cavalry Division Ammtn. Park From 1st March to 31st March 1916		
Heading	War Diary of 2nd Cavalry Division Ammtn Park From 1st to 30th April 1916		
Heading	War Diary of 2nd Cavalry Division Ammtn. Park From 1st May 1916 To 31st May 1916		
War Diary	Avroult	01/05/1916	31/05/1916
Heading	War Diary of 2nd Cavalry Division Ammtn Park From 1st May 1916 to 31st May 1916		
War Diary	Avroult	13/06/1916	20/06/1916
War Diary	Hazebrouck	21/06/1916	30/06/1916
Heading	War Diary of 2nd Cav Div. Ammtn Park From 1st June 30th June 1916. Vol 21		
Heading	War Diary of 2nd Cavalry Divisional Ammunition Park. From: 1st July to 31st July. 1916. (Volume XXIII).		
War Diary	Hazebrouck	01/07/1916	31/07/1916
Heading	War Diary of 2nd Cav. Div. Ammunition Park for August, 1916. Vol		
War Diary	Hazebrouck	01/08/1916	22/08/1916
Heading	War Diary of Ammunition Park, 2nd Cavalry Division for September, 1916. Volume XXV.		
War Diary	Hazebrouck	01/09/1916	05/09/1916
War Diary	S'Venant	06/09/1916	06/09/1916
War Diary	Tangry	07/09/1916	07/09/1916
War Diary	Vacqueritte	08/09/1916	09/10/1916
War Diary	Villers L'Hopital	10/10/1916	10/10/1916
War Diary	Vignacourt	11/10/1916	11/10/1916
War Diary	Nr Le Neiville	12/10/1916	13/10/1916
War Diary	Nr Le Carcaillot Farm	14/10/1916	30/10/1916
Heading	War Diary of 2nd Cavalry Divl. Ammunition Park. October, 1916. Vol. XXVI.		
War Diary	Nr Carcaillot Farm	01/10/1916	07/10/1916
War Diary	Nr Buire	08/10/1916	21/10/1916
War Diary	Buire	22/10/1916	29/10/1916
War Diary	Neville	30/10/1916	31/10/1916
Heading	War Diary of 2nd Cavalry Divisional Ammunition Park. November, 1916. Vol. XXVII.		
Heading	War Diary of 2nd Cavalry Ammtn Park. From 1.11.16. to 30.11.16		
War Diary	Neville	01/11/1916	07/11/1916
War Diary	Bouroon	08/11/1916	08/11/1916
War Diary	Cherienne	09/11/1916	29/11/1916
Heading	War Diary of 2nd Cavalry Divisional Ammunition Park. December, 1916. Vol.27		

Heading	War Diary of 2nd Cav. Ammtn Pk From 1.12.16 To 31.12.16		
War Diary	Cherienne	01/12/1916	31/12/1916
Heading	War Diary of 2nd Cavalry Divisional Ammunition Park. January, 1917. Vol. XXIX.		
Heading	War Diary of 2nd Cav. Ammtn Park. From 1.1.17 To 31.1.17		
War Diary	Cherienne	01/01/1917	31/01/1917
Heading	War Diary of 2nd Cavalry Divisional Ammunition Park. February, 1917. Vol. XXX.		
War Diary	Chenienne	01/02/1917	27/02/1917
War Diary	Guigny	28/02/1917	28/02/1917
Heading	War Diary of 2nd Cavalry Divisional Ammunition Park. March, 1917. Vol. XXXI.		
Heading	War Diary of 2nd Cav. Ammtn Pk. From 1.3.17 to 31.3.117.		
War Diary	Guigny	01/03/1917	05/03/1917
War Diary	Wadicourt	06/03/1917	17/03/1917
War Diary	Tincques	18/03/1917	25/03/1917
War Diary	Wadicourt	26/03/1917	31/03/1917
Heading	War Diary of 2nd Cav. Ammtn Pk From 1.3.17 to 31.3.17.		
Heading	War Diary of 2nd Cavalry Divisional Ammunition Park. Vol. XXXII. April, 1917.		
Heading	War Diary of 2nd Cav. Ammtn Pk From 1.4.17 to 30.4.17		
War Diary	Wadicourt	01/04/1917	06/04/1917
War Diary	Rollecourt	07/04/1917	19/04/1917
War Diary	Henu	20/04/1917	30/04/1917
Heading	War Diary of 2nd Cav. Ammtn Pk. From 1-4-17 to 30-4-17		
Heading	War Diary of 2nd Cav. Ammtn Pk From 1.5.17 to 31.5.17. Vol 32		
War Diary	Henu	01/05/1917	12/05/1917
War Diary	Fouilloy	13/05/1917	13/05/1917
War Diary	Longavesnes	14/05/1917	20/05/1917
War Diary	Tincourt	21/05/1917	31/05/1917
Heading	War Diary 2nd Cav. Ammtn Pk From 1.5.17 to 31.5.17		
Heading	War Diary of 2nd Cavalry. Ammtn Park. From 1st June 1917 To 30th June 1917. (Vol:		
War Diary	Tincourt	01/06/1917	30/06/1917
Heading	War Diary of 2nd. Cavalry. Ammtn Pk From 1st June 1917 To 30th June 1917. (Vol:		
Heading	War Diary of 2nd Cav. Ammtn Pk From 1.7.17 to 31.7.17. Vol 34		
War Diary	Tincourt	01/07/1917	13/07/1917
War Diary	Gouy-En-Ternois	14/07/1917	15/07/1917
War Diary	Gouy	16/07/1917	31/07/1917
Heading	War Diary of 2nd Cav. Ammtn Pk From 1.7.17 To 31.7.17		
Heading	War Diary of No.2 Cavalry Ammunition Park From. 1.8.17. to 31.8.17. Vol 35		
War Diary	Gouy-En-Ternois	01/08/1917	31/08/1917
War Diary	Bethune	17/08/1917	20/08/1917
War Diary	Gouy-En-Ternois	20/08/1917	20/08/1917
War Diary	Gouy-En-Ternois	29/07/1917	29/07/1917

War Diary	Bethune	30/07/1917	17/08/1917
Heading	War Diary of No.2 Cavalry Ammunition Park. From. 1st Sept. 1914. To. 30th Sept. 1914.		
War Diary	Gouy-En-Ternois	01/09/1917	04/09/1917
War Diary	Buneville	05/09/1917	30/09/1917
Heading	War Diary of No.2 Cavalry Ammunition Park. From. 1st. Sept. 1917. To. 30th Sept. 1917.		
Heading	War Diary of 2nd Cav. Div. Ammtn Park From 1st June 1916 To 30th June 1916		
War Diary	Avroult	01/06/1916	12/06/1916

WO 95/11283

Jam Gray Jin Diary

Jam Gray Jin Quemoy Hank
(56 Gay HSC)

1914 AUG - 1917 SEP
To Box 134

2nd CAN DIV Supply

2nd Cavalry Div'l Amm'n Park 121/1364
t / A.C.
Vol. I. 1/5 - 31/8/14

QMG

AG

do. Yesterday fixed up billets for the men. Received
orders at 8 P.M. to move to Amiens next day.

21st August Left Rouen at 7.30 a.m.
Halley Lor: 333. Ran out one big end. Could
not repair so it came on on 3 cylinders.
Halley P.S. 438 cast the off hind tyre. Came on
for 10 miles and then the wheel went & had to
be abandoned 9 miles from Amiens.
Arrived at Amiens at 6 P.M. Not a good
average but it was the first time the Park had
moved as a whole.
Reported to S. of T. First trouble with Hay the
Gunner officer who is only a Sp Special Reserve
I think from the way he talks & acts.
Got an order for two new lorries in exchange for
333 & 438.
Petrol lorry of 5th Div A.T. caught on fire. Of course
no officer on the spot so helped clear the lorry of
Shell.
Received orders for next day. Sent lorry for
rations + out to break down lorry.

22º 12.45 a.m ration lorry returned. 1. a.m. lorry
returned from break down lorries 127, 120 back
56th lorries joined column. Slept in car
Took over charge of caps tractors also
tractors for Army Troops S.C.
Move off at 8 a.m.
Halley Liv. 238 knocking badly but came

42

or empty. Arrived at St Quentin 12-40 PM. No
orders at Post office - Left at 1-15. See lorries going
well on — Lorry No 238.
Arrived Bohain 2-20. No orders so proceeded
to Ramicourt. No orders there. Reported arrival
to C.H.Q. and Supt. Ammunition -
Supt Keston came in with report of tractors. Lorry
tractors past by St Quentin. O.T. S.C. tractor had
dropped trouble plug but was coming on under
Supt Bass.
Received orders to draw supplies at 6.39 a.m. from
Ramicourt station.
Gave verbal orders for no man to leave Column —
at 7.30 posted sentries. Slept in Car.

23rd August. Received orders midnight (22nd) to proceed
in the morning to Aulnoye via Le Cateau &
Landrecies. Started at 7. a.m.
Halley Lorry 238 arrived just as we were moving
off & promptly put a connecting rod through the crank
case thus it is left there.
Lorry to bring on rations was left behind.
At Le Cateau Lorry 59 cast a tyre. Wires too soft
for wheel. Arrived at Aulnoye at 10.45 a.m.
Wired to G.H.Q. & L.of.C.
Lorry W.S. 138 Carburettor caught on fire but was
put out before any damage was done.
Lorry 127 foot brake caught on fire & that was
also put out. 4 P.M. Supt Keston came in

to the tractor reported.
(1) Tractor 5a well on its way.
(2) " " 58. Will [illegible] [illegible] which valve spindle broken at St Quentin.
(3) Halley Lorry Div. 172 had broken its steering gear & gone over a bank 12 miles from Le Cateau - and could not be pulled out even with large tractor. 4.15 P.M. Sent Coy Sergt Major Handy back with lorry to bring in crew & also to bring in Lorry 58.

4.30. Receive orders to stop where I am & to get in touch with [Ammn?] the Column - No operation orders had been given me & no rough idea where any of our troops were. I did not know in which direction to send either N.E or W. I sent Hacker out giving him two scouts & to try & find out if any one knew the direction they were in. He could not get in touch that night - Was lost & upset about the Lorries. Here were my only two 1st aid & Spare lorries broken down & abandoned & I was fully loaded & had to carry besides - Petrol - Rations & spare parts for Lorries & certain coy stores etc an no transport allowed for it. The result was I had to over load - And Lorry 58 with no tyre on had to carry a full load - Each Column or Park however small should have (1) a Petrol Lorry - (2) Ration Lorry (3) One Company Lorry for office spare rifles

44

Stationary [?] & the rumoured some things that the
O.C. Company is held directly responsible for
as parting case of MOPS etc.
On looking over my lorries found the gate change
broke but on one Halley broken so sent Sergt Kestin
to Beaugency to take the one off abandoned lorry —
I was short of Petrol as I had lost all that was
on the lorry that had gone over the bank —

24th August. Hacker returned at 10. a.m. having
found the Ammunition Column. They had not issued
anything — Halley K 169. broke a front spring
found some old material & put on a patch with
two clips — Had a drill parade 7 a.m. for Cat-
C men — No news & no orders —

6.25 a.m. orderly came from A.C. to ask if we
were in the same place to say he had no orders
Aeroplane came down & broke telegraph wires
Troops are moving South but can't find out
what is happening —

25th August. Heard rumours of a retirement but
could get no definite news — A Division
marched South through Aulnaye so telephoned
to G.H.Q. to A.M.G's office — They told us they
knew nothing about us & advised us to get
in touch with the 5th Cav Brigade & act
as I thought best — Sent Hacker out to A.C
which he found just outside Aulnaye
on the way to Traineine so I thought

45

I had better go to Maroilles at which place we arrived at 3 P.M. At 4 P.M an orderly arrived with the order for me to go to Etreux via Landrecies. This order I sh'd have received before 10.a.m. I answered as I was at Maroille & my Colonel had told me they w'd probably require ammunition next day that I would stop where I was unless I received further orders — A Brigade of Infantry & their transport arrived during the afternoon. At 7.P.M. a report that the Germans were 2 miles away came in — The alarm sounded & every one turned out — At 10.30 P.M we were ordered by the Brigade to follow the Horse Transport. No route was given tiny orders were to follow on the last wagon. We started at midnight mean while the firing was on both sides of us & about 400 yards away. The pace was 1 mile an hour & we carried no lights. The road was narrow & bad & the storm we had had during the afternoon had made the roads greasy. Very soon a lorry went into a ditch. We got it out with difficulty. Motor cyclists were useless they could not possibly come up —
At dawn I found only 6 wagons in front of me under a Capt & I had only four lorries behind me — We arrived at Favril where
26th we were told by a priest that the Germans

Suffered in division. I went out to look for my lorries & very nearly got shot at by a Cavalry patrol one of our own. They told me they had seen some lorries in difficulty. So off I went & found they belonged to another division. I returned to Toneil & collected my lorries & proceeded to Etreux, where I arrived at 10. a.m. & found the other lorries had just arrived. I drew supplies & petrol. I was told by Staff Officer where 5th Cav. Brigade was so sent Hacker up there. He returned at 4 P.M. saying we had to go on to St Quentin. We moved off at 4.30 P.M. & arrived there at 8 P.M. Hacker also reported that the Cavalry would not require ammunition for 3 days.

27th August. It rained all night.
5.15 a.m. Staff Officer Q.M.G. Staff arrived & told me to move at once to Roisby. I did so but did not get there till 8 a.m. as the road was blocked.
At 11 a.m. had orders to move on to Cugny. Found 2nd Div: Amm Park there.

28th August at 1. a.m. I heard the other Park moving & found they had orders to move. So I moved off at 2 a.m. & arrived at Chauny where I found petrol & supplies + ~~2nd Div~~ Cav Div: S.C. waiting to load.

28th August Cont. I was then ordered to move to ~~Mus~~ Manicampo.
At 2. P.M. Col Gilpin arrived & told me to send in to Compiegne at 9 P.M. for orders.
Hacker went off as directed.

29th August
2. A.m Hacker returned with no orders as there were none to be issued. He was very fed up, over 90 kilometres night riding for no object is enough to make any one fed. Hacker is the hardest working fellow I have come across & has more common sense than most people & can always be trusted to do the right thing if left in charge.
4.30 a.m Major Percival arrived & ordered 1 Lorry 13 pr & 1 Lorry S.A.A to be sent to 3rd Cav Brigade. He gave me the order in writing as I was the 5th
Hacker took them off.
I bought 1100 kilograms of coal for tractors for 1st Cav Div S.C. & 4th Div S.C. at least I gave a requisition price 55 fr. Sent Sgt Keates to am Colm which I hear is at Simeny. He returns & say they require ammunition at 3.30 P.M.
Off load 57 cases S.A.A. & 3 cases 13 pr & certain gun parts. We then proceed to ~~via centre~~ Compiegne

Report to ... as yet promised two lorries
next day - Draw 2500 francs from Coplin
& get bed 2 a.m.

30th August. Hear that Hewson lorries have
already been ordered to Crépy - Try to draw
ammunition but that has been sent off -
Leave at 3 P.M -
Halley Lio 317 strips timing wheel on
magneto shaft have to be abandoned - Luckily
I get two from Hewson at Crépy -
We arrive at Nanteuil at 9 P.M. & draw
our ammunition a stop there the night - Our
orders were to go to Nanteuil & then to Coulommes

31st 6. a.m escorted loads. Moved off to
Coulommes on arrival there found we were
up with Head Qrs Cav Brigade - As there
were several lorries I wanted to dismantle
I got permission to go back to Nanteuil
Karrier broke rear spring rear suspension
bracket & the load had to be taken off -
Halley Lio 167 broke both front springs
the old hands and the other springs too
Leyland 59 had done 200 miles without
a tyre & the wheel was every thing but in
& every spoke was cracked. So I was
in a bad way & was two short of
actual carrying weight not counting
petrol & stores etc -

121/3905

2nd Cavy. Div: Ammn Park.

Vol II. 5.10 — 31.12.14

2nd Cav. Div. Am.n Park

5th October No move.

6th October moved at 8.7 a.m to Ailly sur Noye
arrived 10 a.m.

7th October Moved at 7.a.m arrived Amiens at
10 a.m

8th October No move.

9th October Moved at 3 P.M. to Picquiny
Halford tr.IV. 309 over a 20 ft. drop at
Talmas with broken steering — could not
move it.

10th October reported to D of T. + Hacker drew
a new lorry.

11th October Left at 7.a.m arrived Blangy
10. a.m.
Sergt Kirstin had accident returning from
Column — admitted to French Convent.

12th October Hacker went to Abbeville to
obtain pass ports.

13th October Left 8.a.m arrived Wardrecques
at 11.30 a.m. £3 lorries 13 passengers
at Castre — returned too late to refill

14th October Park ordered to Castre but
when we got there we were ordered to return

15th October D: Anderson joined Park.

16th October
17th October } No move.

18th October I took 6 lorries to Wytschaete
Hacker took H⁴ gun to Strazeele.

19th October I went to Column.
   Hacker took up am⁴⁰ at 3 P.M.

20th October Anderson took up 5 lorries ord⁵
   to go to Wytschaete but column had to
   move back to Kemmel. return S at 12 m.m.

21st October Am⁴⁰ ran out at Railhead
   requires 5 lorry loads. 45 tons
   left unloaded. 4 lorries to Column.

22nd October Still no am⁴⁰ 13 pr. +
Column requires five loads.
Park ordered to Ebblinghem. Borrowed
four lorries of 13 pr. from 1st C.A.P. who
had more than their full amount.
Same arrived at 3 P.M. & I took up
5 lorries to La Clytte leaving Caestre
at 4.30. Did not arrive at La Clytte
till 11.30 P.M. owing to road being

blocked by Motor Lorries with Indian Troops
left Harcher up with Column as they did not
require it all that night. I returned to
Ebblinghem & found Col Seymour waiting there.
with report that Column had no accident.

23rd Oct. No move.

24th Oct.   "

25th Oct. C.S.M. took up two lorries.

26th Oct. Sent a pair of Halley Wheels to
          Paris.

29th Oct. Moved to Itogenle — Saw Major Wilder

30th Oct. Returned to Ebblinghem & Parked at
          Reneseure. Sent 8 lorries to la Clytte

31st Oct. L. Bray arrived — with no kit or any thing
          3 Douglas bicycles arrived.
          Sent Pte White to live with Column in
          case they moved.
          Andrew went up with 7 lorries at 2 P.M.
          returned at 11.30 P.M.

1st Nov. Hacker took 6 lorries to Reninghelst
had been up to the Column with Gibbons
returned with Hacker.

2d Nov: Anderson took up 4 lorries did not
return till 12 n.n.

3d Nov. Hacker took up three lorries.

4th Nov. Received new Halley springs which
did not fit my 3 Ton chain Halleys.

5th Nov. Moved to Steazeele
Two lorries under C.S.M to Column.
Two lorries left at Reninn... under
slight repairs + one with wheels which
had been sent to Paris.

6th Nov. Moved to Morbecque.

7th Nov. Divided the Park into No 1 No 2.
workshop sects.
Hacker went to Talmas to bring in
the engine of L.N. 309.

8th Nov. Drill parade.

9th Nov. Hacker returned.
Rec'd 2 Rear Halley wheels ⎫ 1st
2 Front " " ⎬ Cap.
1 " Dennis " ⎭

10th Nov Drills.

11th Nov Andrew took up amm[unition]

12th Nov. two lorries went up.
13th Nov. Lt Nisbet joined

14th Nov. Hacker took up broken wing to
            Neuve Eglise.

15th Nov. two sets of Halford wheels sent to
            Paris

16th & 18th Nov Two lorries sent up daily
            under sealed orders from 12th each
            sent alternately.

19th Nov Moved to Hazebrouck. Snow & frost —
            roads in bad state.

20th Nov. Bombs fell near Park aimed
            at Railway station. Heavy frost.
            2 lorries arrived with 15 pr amm[unition]
21st Nov Still freezing — 3 pumps broken

22nd Nov. One Halford Cylinder cracked —
            Sent up one lorry small arms —

23rd Nov. Wheels arrive for Halley at
            Renescure — find one cylinder cracked
            wire to Ad: M.T. Base.

Find out an acetylene process in S'
Order. Send Hacker to fix up to have
both cylinders done.
Darimlar bursts three tubes in radiator.
24th Nov. No more casualties in lorries.
Have charcoal burning between lorries.
26th Nov. Thaw starts.
26th Nov. Go on leave to England.
28th Nov. Park moves to Vieux Berquin
 NCO's go on leave.
30th Nov. Return from leave & Major
 Gibbon goes on leave.

1st Dec. Hacker & Andrews go on leave.
   Have a lot of office work to do.
2nd Dec. Orders received for Hacker to report
   to Commandant Boulogne on 6th
   obtain permission for him to report
   in England.
3rd Dec. Rifle inspection - write in about
   Coy Sergt Major Hardy's promotion.
   wire to Hacker.
4th Dec. to 12th Dec.
   Parades for provisional ranks.
   engines overhauled - received ammunition
13th Dec. Went to Rouen for spare gear
   wheels for Daimler car.
14th Dec. Returned from Rouen.
21st Dec. Report arrival of 2nd Lieut Boulton
   14 of the men, myself get inoculated.
23rd Dec. General Boyce inspects the Park
   Lorries covered in mud - certain tyres
   to be changed.
24th Dec. All lorries washed - get
   two sets of tyres changed. None of the
   other sizes available.
26th Dec. Go to G.H.Q. with weekly state.
   Report received at Div. HQ re state
   of the Park.

27th Statios etc. Burlton arrives having had accident with Sunbeam. Send lorry to tow it in.

28th Go to R.H.Q with list of lorries etc.
Parade 9.15 to 11.
See P.K.G. who has been told to inspect Park. Rubury returns from leave.

29th Nisbet goes to St Omer to buy some white metal.
Parade. Gibbon returns from leave.
Anderson goes on leave.

30th Receive orders to send two Karriers + one Leyland to G.H.Q + bring back Halleys.
Also to send Wolseley to Lahore S. pol, Colm.
Following Halleys received - 16A - 3907 - 3341 -
Innoculated for second time.
Parade - Foot drill -

31st Triumph Motor bicycle put under cover had been lying in the road for days & parts gradually disappearing. Reported to Signals as it is believed to belong to them.
Wolseley sent to Lahore Supply Colum.
Sunbeam Car No 806 sent to R.T.O. to be forwarded to Paris for repair.
Monthly states sent to D D of T, J.G.C. to D of T. + Cav Div.

G.E. Goldsmith Capt
ASC
K 2 Cav Div An'x Park

121/4261.

2nd Cavy: Div: Annual Report.

Vol III. 1 — 31.1.15

1915.

1st January. 1915. Received wire from England to say L/Cpl Randall C had been admitted to H whilst on 72 hrs leave. Drill parade under L⁺ Burlton. Lorries cleaned up Park put straight.

2nd Jan. 9.30 a.m. Col Franks inspected Park. Made out states. Took them into G.H.Q. Gunpowder demanded by R.E. none at Argus Road march.

3rd Jan. Parade 9.30 a.m. Make out orders for Orderly Officer. Make out Sunday states + ammⁿ return. Draw 100 lbs gunpowder S⁺ Vernon. Draw 4000 francs. 7 men go on leave.

4th Jan. Receive orders to send following lorries.
  Albion to 3rd C.A.P.
  Thornycroft to 2 A.P.
  Hallford to 1 C.A.P.
  2 Ton Hallford to G.H.Q.
Also Wolseley to Lahore S.C. but this was done on 31-12-14.
Make out orders for Orderly Sergt.
Albion returns as 3. C.A.P have no Hallfps wire to D of T.
Ration Lorry gets ditched send out Burlton

at 7.P.M. Report that none of T. officers are
fit to command Supply Columns of Am.t Parks
Parade 9.a.m. — Marching parade 2.P.M.
5th Jan. Giblin leaves park to join K's Army.
 receive orders to send Daimler to Lahore S.C.
 Halley 1118 arrives in place of Thorncroft from
 2 AP. Drill 9.30 and Marching Parade 2.P.M.
 Halley No. 3638 arrived from GHQ to took Holford No 1284
6th Jan. In bed with bad cold. Flu —
 Anderson returns from leave — Daimler Car broken down
7th Jan. Got up about mid day but did not go out —
 Halley No. 63 & No. 3029 arrived under officer
 1st Ind Cav Am.t Park. Halley No 63 he had taken over
 from 2 AP. He had orders to take two Albions
 from me but as I have only one & that was ordered
 to 3. C. AP. I did not give it. Wired to D of T.
 Nisbet goes on leave —
8th Jan. The lorries from 1st Ind Cav — no lamps
 etc — Get new lorries washed down. Parades
 daily 9.30 a.m & 2.P.M —
 Have two targets made — Fever towards night
9th Jan — Wire picked up & given in from D of T.
 ordering Albion to be sent to 1st Ind Cav
 Am.t Park. Sent Rubury in with Stah to DDofT
 only 26 lorries owing to changes — 9 men go on
 leave — Have to borrow money to pay out —
 owe POM — 100 francs — Some forty odd
 men got inoculated after Maj McCallan

had spoken to them.

10th Jan. Church Parade 11-30 a.m.
Send names of men with no numbers to Records O.A.
11th Jan. Exchange damaged wheel with 3 Cdn. of
Trun: M.B. Go to St. Omer for spares - get
12 Halford Piston rings - on to Camp shows -

12th Jan. Receive Halley No. 16 - from 1st 2nd Cdn
Aux. Park - all lorries greased etc.
Go to Wizernes to look for billets - very hard
can't find sitting room nor office -
14 Drivers, 1 fitter turner arrive from Base.
No papers with them - Two no numbers -

13th Jan. Go to Cav. Corps Hd. Qrs. then to G.H.Q. A lot
of spare parts for Halley arrive at St. Omer
Orders received not to move to Wizernes till
Saturday 16th. Doctors certificate received from
Piper in England -
14th Jan. Distribute drivers to lorries. Send in
reminder re Anderson's commission. Forward
state to DADT I.G.C. - large consignment of Halley
spare parts arrive. Draw 4000 francs -
Paid back Pom 100 francs
15th Jan. See Col. Longmore re report on 2nd Bray
Anderson pays out the Park 3220 francs
10 N.C.O.'s & men go on leave - order read

on the two parades re fast driving + penalty.
Lt Nisbet returns from leave.

16th Jan Get Lorries on the move at 9.a.m. to go to
Wizernes. Meet three Lorries on a narrow bit of
road + it takes 1½ hours to push them past.
I go on to G.H.Q. with return — Find Park
parking in yard of paper mill — Can get them
all in except Petrol Lorry, which is left on
the side of the road — Halford 226 bumped
another lorry + smashed radiator. Three of
the new Halleys require new clutch leathers.
Officers billets 400 yds from Park.

17th Jan Have Latrines dug + general clean
up + wash down — Report on Beay forwarded
to D of T. Sunday returns made out. Have
orders to move my park so that S.C. can get
through their workshops — Send Edwards on
motor bicycle to Rouen with return of fitters
NCO's.

18th Jan. Send for 156,000 rounds S.A.A. to complete
Park from Strazeele — Send Nisbet to Isbergue
re tyres — Receive Daimler Car in place
of Sunbeam. Receive copy of D of T.'s report.

19th Jan. Three Halleys received from G.H.Q.
Nos 6087-8-9 — in place of Halfords
900 - 203 - 349 — Parades as usual.

20th Janu. See Site for range send in application with rough sketch for permission to fire —
Receive order to exchange 15 pr. War: H.A attached to 1st Army. No place given so send it back to D.H.Q. for more detail — AA & M.G. asked for 150 rifle grenades + 3000 blank. Only 35 on Park & few at Railhead by OO will not issue without G.H.Q. authority — Capt Davidson inspects Park —

21st Janu. At 12-30 P.M. orders come down to send 15 pr. to War. H.A at Vieille Chapelle. Rubury takes it and leaves at 1. P.M — They require 319 rounds 545 fuzes — Gottwaltz goes to draw the latter. Too wet for parades. Rubury returns at 2.15 a.m. having issued 264 rounds complete on all 600 fuzes — Anderson takes Karrier 48 to G.H.Q + Leyland 59 to 2. A.P. & brings back two Halleys 910 from latter — returns at 10 P.M — 10 men go on leave.

22nd Jan — Column require 434 rounds shell — Ammunition Railhead still at Strazeele — Two Halleys 930. H1502 arrive from 1st A.P. Re lorries sent to Isbergues No 679 — for new tyres breaker down + another has to be sent out to tow it in — No 679 . received from 2 AP rather a D u D — Give orders to empty radiators —

23rd Jan Heavy frost last night — Halley No. 6072 from G.H.Q for repair in exchange for Dennis New Tyres for Hallford 226 come back.
Go to G.H.Q with State — Draw 4000 Francs from F.C.

24th Jan: Permission is given to make a rifle Range - which we proceed to do - Burlton returns from leave. New numbers 5540 to 5560 is given to the Park - Tyre 1010 x 120 sent to Isbergue returns same day. This is the only type they can do there -
Receive wire to send 3 Halfords to 1. A.P. and 2 Halfords to 6. A.P. in exchange for Halleys - wire to D of T only four Halfords & one requires new timing case cover -

25th Jan D of T's wire cancelled - Column ask for 362.000 rounds S.a.a + 4000 rounds Revolver - Rubury takes it up + Anderson refils - returns 10.30 P.M. The men start firing. Some very bad -

26th Jan. Strazeele can retype on Thursday - 830 x 120 Fore - 850 x 100. Hind - Two Halleys received from 1st A. P. in place of 2 Halfords - 222. 223 - Hand over some Thornycroft + Leyland spares to 2d A.P. - 6 N.CO's to be sent to England to re'army -

28th Jan. Three Halleys arrive from G.H.Q for my last two Halfords and Leyland. Two men drunk - Five NCO's start for Havre - Payout - Send tyres to Strazeele to be retyred -

29th Jan. Give Burchett 28 day No 1 for Drunk } See them
     "   Henley 14 ————————— } 6 a P.M.
O/c Press Strazeele returns front wheel of No. 5341 as not wanting to be retyred - Draw 3000 Francs from Field Cashier - Cpl Cosgrove goes to Havre on duty yesterday today -

Sent up shell to Warickshire H.A.

30th Jan - Go to P.H.Q. with state - Refil 15 pr. Lorry steering given out. Receive orders for move on Monday morning - Send off for Very's revolver amm'n. O.O. will not issue as we are in reserve. Pt. Williams sent in as prisoner Hans'd Over -

31st Jan. Four lorries dismantled when order to move comes in. Two bad steering, will have to tow - two engines down for big ends etc.

Sent in returns for the week and for the end of the month - Returns for A.O.D.T & I.G.C. by motor cyclists -

O.O. issues 240 rounds asked for 3000 - of Very's flares -

C.L. Goldsmith Capt
A.S.C
O.C. 2" Cavalry Amm Park

1/2/15

$\frac{121}{4468}$

2nd Ass't Dis't Attorn'y Pub.

Vol IV 1-28-2-15

68

February 1915.

1st Feb. Park moves off at 12.45 P.M. and arrives at Vieux-Berquin at 4.P.M. Road from Hazebrouck congested. All lorries except two (one towing another) in by 5. P.M. Several small things wrong. Coy Q.M.S. Lynn went to No 2 Reserve Park yesterday on probation to S.M.

2nd Feb. Send diary to D.A.G. Base. Go to Argues about rifle grenades & very's pistol cartridges for trial. Men return from leave.

3rd Feb. Daimler fears M961 gone again. Receive word of B 213 (a.s.c. new War Establishment – notice I am two motor cycles under establishment. Have to send states etc to A. & S.T. now instead of M of T. also copies of B 213. more office work.

4th Feb. Issue rifle grenades etc to the 3rd Brigade. 10 Sail covers at G.H.Q.

5th Feb. Issue 76,000 S.a.a

6th Feb. Issue 46,750 S.a.a + 200,000 S.a.a. Have to withdraw Rifle grenades & hand over to 1st C.D. & 3rd C.D. 4 + 9 respectively. Later have to withdraw very's pistol ammn as 3rd C.D. are short in trenches. Send

1 lorry to refill. See a.d. S+T. in place
of D. of S+T.

7th Feb. Issue 168 buys to 3rd C.D. & 9 grenades.
Send three lorries to Arques for 229.000 to
complete. See Col Franks to arrange re
trench bombs while 2nd C.D. are in the trenches.
Arrange to detach one Lorry.

Drew 229.000 rounds S.a.a. — Set of sprocket
brackets not at G.H.Q. railhead as advised.

8th Feb Send Leyland Lorry 57 to G.H.Q. Go to G.H.Q. re
stores.

9th Feb. Send in requisition for tools to complete lorries.
See Col Franks. Have to send five lorries to Poperinghe
for Am.n while div. in the trenches in place of Am.n
Column.

10th Feb. Col Longmore arrived to see me about sending
a representative to Arques every day. Braund
to hand over 400.000 S.a.a to 3rd C.D. at 4 P.M.
tomorrow.

11th Feb. Issue 708, 13 pr. & 48.000 S.a.a to a.m.Col.
Take over 234 650 rounds S.a.a. from 3rd Cav Brigade
"   "   49 900 ——————— 12th Lancers.
         70 500 ——————— 20th Hussars.
         91 200 ——————— 3"   "
         30 000 ——————— Scots Greys.
         28 000 ——————— 6" D.G.
         67 120 ——————— Oxford Hussars.
         ~~6720~~
         571,370 ———————

Hand over 600 650 rounds S.A.A to 3rd C.D. A.P.
A lot of the S.A.A handed back by units is loose
and in sacks. Send one lorry to R.E to take up bombs.
Sentries arrest a man about 11 P.M. but I let him
go as he is evidently a refugee looking for a
place to sleep.

12th Feb. Send two lorries 4th Bde Head Qrs
one lorry to 3rd B. Head Qrs. to take up kits etc. to
Poperinghe. Two lorries to go to 5th Brigade tomorrow
same time viz 9 a.m. Anderson will be in
charge of these lorries and collect the Amm't at
Poperinghe where the 3rd Cav Div has left it.

13th Feb. Render returns + see A.D.O.S. +T. Am't Park
to carry out light repairs to ambulances.
At 2 P.M. hear that transport arrangements
to carry stake over the Am't at Poperinghe have
gone astray. It afterwards comes out that
billeting area have been changed but I was
not notified. A.A & M.G under impression
that I see operation orders.
Draw following from Argues. 120 Granades
hand with detonators + 360 vey flares.
At 11 P.M. receive wire from field Squadron
F.E for 5000 sand bags.

14th Feb. Draw 4000 francs. Send bomb lorry to

Struggle for sand bags & then on to Hazebrouck
to go up with Supply Column.
Anderson takes over from 3 C.o.P. 399,800 rnds
800 .99 Rifle grenades complete.
295 Hand grenades complete.
283 yds Instantan: Fuze.
15 Periscopes. 13 Fathoms Safety Fuze.
1 Rammer.
6 Boxes Webley Pistol.
Lorry sent to Arques drew. 102 Hand grenades complete
304 Bombs 9 5"M.M. 56 Safety Fuze. 360 Verys.

15th Feb. Bomb lorry sent up Indent for R.E. Stores
arrives about mid-night & 100,000 rounds S.A.A required
Stores drawn at 7. a.m. I leave with four lorries at
9 a.m. Arrive at Poperinghe and collect bomb
lorry from S! Jean ter Biezen. See Col Franks.
Go on to Ypres and hand over barbed wire, Corragates
Iron, bombs Flares etc. No more grenades required
for the time being. Leave another lorry with
Anderson as one lorry has broken a radius
rod. Return at 8.P.M. Roads very bad and
weather vile. Wire netting required but none
at R.E. Park Struggle. S.A.A & M.G. purchases
some set is sent up to Ypres at 4 PM by
Car. Advance section have to send in S.A.A
to Ypres daily by 6P.M. Only small

amounts required — No orders yet received about the 1000 rounds handed into Pack Regt reserve —

16th Feb. Draw more RE Stores & one lorry sent to join Supply Column at Hazebrouck at 8 am written instructions given to L/Cpl Turner NCO i/c. — Two lorries to be handed over for 13pr amm<u>n</u> for Warwickshire Horse Artillery —

Pay out — Acting rants are very keen —
5000 sand bags required but none at RE Railhead — Two trailers arrive for 13pr amm<u>n</u> — Stores M.T. arrive G.H.Q.

17th Feb. Send 600 Very flares up to Ypres by car. Field Squadron wire for 15000 sand-bags but none are available —

13pr: amm<u>n</u> limited to 8 rounds per gun per day when in action — but account can be kept as a running account 144 rounds per day — Sent lorry to draw bombs at Argues.

18th Feb. Send bomb lorry to Hazebrouck to join up with Supply Column — No sand bags at Strazeele wire to 2 Cos to that effect —
At mid-day 6000 sand bags arrive for 2 Cos. at Strazeele which I send up —
Anderson sends down two lorries &
170.000 rounds & 20 boxes of Revolver amm<u>n</u> are sent up — Orders received that Regt reserve dumped with me can be used by me.

19th Feb. Send to Argues for Bombs. Send Nisbet
to ●d- Omer to buy angle iron for Bale Hoops.
Two Douglas motor cycles arrived yesterday.
Issue one to each section. Have to train the
N.C.O's to ride. Issue 5000 sand bags to
2d Field Squadron. Send up 85,000 rounds S.A.A

20th Feb. Return all hand grenades to Argues
also all loose & open boxes of S.A.A.
Gottwaltz goes to Ypres. Detail for return of Brigade
sent to Anderson. Return of explosives etc sent
to A.D.M.C. Send in State.

21st Feb. Send up 3000 sand bags. 4 boxes light ball
1 Box detonators. 6 Boxes Bombs for Mortars.
Amt. return sent in now to show 13pr. H.E
or Shrapnel. Pte Williams absent from
18th inst.
Amount of Hand grenades sent to Argues
was 246 – with detonators.
Sent by Sergt Major to 2d Field Squadron to
let them know what I was sending up next
day & to ask if that was sufficient.
Answer came back that is was but what
they wanted was hair trigger bombs.
But none are available.
At 5 P.M. a wire came in from Argues
signed A.Q.M.G 2 Cav Div. ordering me to
send a lorry to draw 600. grenades hand

70 Tonite, 300 bombs Mortar wanted at
Zoes tonight. ~~sent~~ ~~via~~ ~~the~~ ~~lorry~~
~~returning~~ send L. Cpl Smith
Back axle for Daimler Car arrives —

22ⁿᵈ Feb. Sent lorry to Hazebrouck to join Supply
Column with — 5000 sand bags,
600 very cartridges, 16m detonators, 16
fathoms Safety fuse & 96 Bombs for Mortar —
Anderson sent down on 21ˢᵗ a lorry for
80000 rounds S.A.A.

N.C.M. wire received urgently required. 5000
sandbags. 300 Bombs mortar, 200 Tin can
Bombs, 500 detonators 5 tins safety fuse,
2 Barrels gun powder 50 steel loop-hole plates.
Send one lorry with 5000 sand bags, detonators, fuse
& plates. No gun powder available & send
one lorry to Aigues to draw Bombs 100 Tin can
bombs available —

L. Cpl Smith returns at mid-day —

Made tests to reduce the glare of head lamps
at night from blinding on coming
vehicle drivers — Tests prove that to blacken
~~the 3 o'clock to 6 o'clock quarter~~ of the 12 to 3 o'clock
quarter of glass, & 6 to 9 o'clock quarter of
reflector cutting out a small circle in the
centre gives the most satisfactory results
with regards to both drivers — ⊖ glass.

23rd. Send J. Birtchell to Ypres with gun powder which has arrived at R E Park Stroquele in their Car.

Pte Williams is brought back at 11.30 a.m. as prisoner by the Military Police — The medical officer detains him as I sent him in for observation —

Order came in for 200 primers gun cotton. No size or weight given. Send them up by motor cyclist luckily obtained the right ones —

Anderson returns —

24th Feb. Anderson handed over 407,680 rounds S.a.a. by 2nd Cav Div: Lorries not in till early morning — Pay C/1318 Pte S.J. Wright the sum of £10 (260 francs) as Class I National Reservist on 24-2-15. on A.F.N R.1. and N.1573 also showed it in A.B.64. Send Anderson to Cassel to draw Amm from 1st C.A.P. at Cassel. Send in report re head lamps. b.o.r. a.s.c. —

M/032905 Pte Dyson J. died in H from ulcers — First case in the Park —

Anderson takes over 343,000 rounds S.a.a. from 1st C.A.P. — Pte Williams was transferred to No. 2 Clearing Casualty Station. Bailleul.

76

26th–7?. 722,800 rounds S.A.A in park of which
1500 is loose.

List of wood used whilst at Vieux Berquin in
making sides & leaves for lorries.
2³/₄" × 7" × 2·86′. 3½" × 2½" × 2·47′. 1½" × 8" × 80′
1 × 9 × 63. × 1 × 7" × 57. ½" × 7½" × 17½′ deal.
Pine. 3" × 9" × 6½′. Price. 152.15 francs.
Issue to 3rd Cav. Brigade. 232,900 Rounds
S.a.a to complete.
I am to issue direct to the other units
when we get into our new billeting area.

26th Feb. Orders received for Park to move off
at 1.30 p.m. 27th inst for Wizernes via
Hazebrouck + Aire. Send two lorries
with Head Quarters to BLENDECQUES and
then to go on to Aire + draw 170,000 s.a.a
return to BLENDECQUES.

27th Amm.n Railhead moved to Arques so
draw 255,000 Saa to fill up units.
Leave Vieux-Berquin at 1.30 P.M. arrive
Wizernes at 3.40 P.M. a good run. One
radius rod bent. 2nd radius rod
that has gone in one week. No
solution at present why this should
happen.

28th. Sent in returns for end of the month & week. Base reports me, for not sending in B213 for 20", to division. A?? gave me instructions not to do so. So will leave them to fight it out. Handed back 11 Parsons Nos. 124 to 126 Nos 17, 18, 20, 21, & 115.

Slight fire broke out in one of the lorries. Small damage done — It was quickly put out by the fire hand extinguishers.

G. Goldsmith Capt
A.S.C.
O.C. 2nd ?id Div. Am't Park.

13/15

12/4/79

A6

121/4779

2nd Cas: Dis l'Amm'n Park.

Vol V 1 – 31.3.15

D.A.G. 3rd Echelon
Base

Herewith my diary for the
month of March 1915.

G. R. Goldsmith Capt
ASC
O.C. 2 Cos Div. Am't Park

1/4/15.

Wizernes

1

1st March Monday. Send diary for Feb to
D.A.C. Base. The damage done by fire
was 1 great coat fur lined - 2 Blankets &
one waterproof sheet. Send copy of aff B 213
for 20th & 27th Feb to O/c A.S.C. Records.
The gears on daimler Car M 1910 have
all gone. The gears seem to be very soft.
Wire for new back axle. Wire base for
refills for fire hand extinguishers.
Parades as usual - drill at 9.30 am. Route
march at 2. P.M. Lieut Burlton orderly officer.

Nisbet goes to St Omer to purchase enough
angle iron 400 ft. to complete my lorries
with bale Hoops. A T/S of A/T now repudiates
having told me not to send aff B. 213 to
O/c Records. Office work very heavy at
present now we have OC. A.S.C. as the
division asks me for a return and then
the O/C. A.S.C. calls for the same return.

One water jacket on lorry 5551 slightly
cracked. No passes available at A.P.M.
so have to make out temporary ones
myself. Now we have left Vieux Berquin
The Army Railhead has been moved to
Strazeele. They always seem to give
us at least a 25 mile run.
The 4th & 5th Brigades have not yet asked
for their ammunition so have all my
spare lorries loaded. So have had to
dump one load to enable me to send a
lorry to St Omer for the angle iron.

2nd March Tuesday.   Wizernes.

2'Lieut Rubury orderly officer.

Receive orders to send one lorry to Wizernes station to report to the D.O.O for the conveyance of R.E Stores. Lorry to be there at 11 a.m.

Send in officers claims yesterday for Field Lodging Fuel & Light. Receive passes (16) numbers C 520 to C 535.

Receive from M.T. ad. Base. 24' Belting 1 Sheet Klingerite 6 tyre repair outfits & 27 pyrene extinguishers.

Report verbally that 4th & 6th Brigades have not asked for their amm⁴ Rgt reserve.

M.T. Base can not supply complete back axle for Daimler - returned box as M.T. depot - 1 sheet Klingerite - 6. Tyre repair outfits on Truck No. . . . not known.

2 P.M. Fatigue party sent to improve the range shooting where we were here before.

Indent for stores a.o.o returned as in excess of a.f G 1098 - 98.

One of the lorries catch on fire in the carburettor owing to a back fire. It was quickly put out with some pyrene extinguishers

3rd March Wednesday – Wizernes   3

Lieut Anderson Orderly Officer. Send one
lorry to Blendecques to a M G's at 9 a m
to be rationed for two days to bring back R E
stores from Ypres. to take extra petrol.

Lieut Anderson Orderly officer. Parade
at 9.30 am.

Another lorry required today at Wizerne Station
at 8 am to carry planks.

Following S.A.A. sent out – asked for.
42 000 rounds. 12th Lancers at AUDINCTHUN
71 000   "   20th Hussars at FAUQUEMBERGUES

Wire to OC A.S.C. M.T. Base for gear wheels for
Daimler 1910 & to advise them of the stores
arriving. Write to sect. officers about
testing their lorries.

2.P.M. 15 men start musketry – five
rounds at 100x 5 rounds at 200x. under
Lieut Boulton. Write to Paymaster Base
re Certificate No.8 Ord-Acc. for 127-50 Francs
for meat punch and bill lost. also re
claims for officers.

Amt. actually drawn. by units.

   20th Hussars.   85 000 rounds
   12th Lancers.   75 000 "

4th March. Thursday – Wizernes. 4

Report due today already sent in to OC ase
de Camp blinding the approaching driver –

Lieut Nisbet orderly officer –

One lorry to draw R.E Stores from Strozule –

Following N.C.O's confirmed in their rank &
to be sent to Havre –
   Sergt Howes, Parkinson, Cpl Randall C
   Randall W, Leavitt J E, Peterson, 2 Cpls
   Ptes Edwards F & Ashton –

Schedule for week sent up to Supply Officer

Div. Troops for countersignature –

Draw 2000 Francs from Field Cashier. He
had no more –

Pay out at 3.30 P.M. as far as the money will
go – 18 men on muster at 2. P.M. Shooting
on the whole bad –

A lot of dissatisfaction over the promotions
of the men sent home O/c Records has
not confirmed any ranks except of the
men sent home. All N.C.O's ask to be
sent home as they are given another step
apparently as soon as they get home.
All the Sergts in 56 Coy before the war are
W.O's because they have left the Coy. The
Coy Sergt Major has not been promoted
because he has done all the hard work
& stopped with the Coy –

5th March Friday - Wizernes. 5

Send in return of Bills to Supply officer -
Send in a report re drivers of Cars to OC A.S.C
Lieut Burlton orderly officer -
Wire to OC M.T. at Depot for cover for water jacket
for lorry 5741 - Issue 4 bores Revolver auto
600 - 18/8/14 - 300 - 22/8/14 - 276 - 7/10/14 to
the 12th Lancers - Drew 2000 Francs from
Paymaster - Issued 8560 S.a.a to
O.C Oxfordshire Hussars,
9 NCO's left for Havre L/Cpl Hollanby
was sent in place of Cpl Randall W.
Payout - 4225 francs A.S.C. 470 R.F.A
20 R.A.M.C Lorry returned last night
from 2puis - Musketry at 2.P.M.
All lorries are being tested up a
steep hill - Only received 5 towing ropes
invoice said 16 towing ropes five tail
lamps. Wire to Records about the departure
of NCO's.

6th March. Saturday. Wizernes.
Orderly officer Lieut Ribury.
25% of explosives required by each field
squadron to be carried by the Am⁵ Column.
Draw the amount from Stazeele.
Make out States. Confirm ranks to fill
up vacancies caused by NCO's going
to England.
R.E. ~~Park~~ F.S. require 500 Ammonal Hand bombs
+ 200 gun bombs send to Stazeele.
Send Rueltin to A⋅D⋅of⋅S⋅+T with state.
R.E Park has only gun bombs.

Aa + A M.G. asks for 60 rifle grenades
for practise. Am⁵ Railhead won't issue
without authority from G.H.Q.
All explosives are issued to Column
except one Exploder + Solution
India rubber. No parade this morning
too wet.

7th March Sunday. Wizernes

Lieut Anderson orderly officer.
Send lorry to Am'n column with explosives
+ car to 2nd Field Squadron with gun
bombs. 6 Towing chains received which
belong to 2nd Indian Cav. wire to Base
+ to 2 Ind Cav. Been very wet for two days
no foot drill parade this morning.

AA & QMG 2nd Cav Div came at 4.30 P.M.
to see the Park. He offered no comments either
good, bad or indifferent.

Receive Schedule 4 from Supply officer.
Circular letter received from DOTS to say
that governors on lorries are not to be touched.
Make out indent for Stationary.
Gottwaltz see Warwickshire R.H.A. about the
number of unserviceable fuses for 15 pr.
330 drawn from Railhead in Jan and
only 92 returned. Re remained still
kept so that serviceable ones need not be
used until required.

8th March Monday. Wizernes.

Lieut Nisbet orderly officer –

Pte Burchett absent off parade at 8 a.m.

Pte Townsborough drunk in Wizerne at 7.30 P.M. 7th Inst.

Wrote to O.C. A.S.C. ask what cases he wishes to deal with –

Send imprest Acc to Command Paymaster with receipts + N 1373 –

Send 100 rounds Revolver to No 9. Mob. Vet. Sect. + the 6 towing wires to 2nd Ind Cav Amm Park to aire –

OC ASC does not wish any cases referred to him – give Townsborough 14 day No 1 Field Punishment – Burchett I gave a chance and admon –

Musketry as usual – and also parade at 9.30 a.m.

The Oxford Hussars hand in unserviceable tripods, maxim gun spare parts 60 w 4 spare barrels + 11 belt boxes –

Sh'd be sent to DOO 2 Cav Div

9th March Tuesday - Wizernes.

Lieut Burlton Orderly Officer -
Have musketry at 9.30 am.
One lorry detailed for Div: Hd Qrs to move
the Hd Qrs to Vieun Berguin - Orders received
that Div: will move today less Ammo
Park which will move on Wednesday to be
at Vieun Berguin at 12 noon -
Lorries to be at Hd Qrs at 9 am - One lorry for
R.E Field Squadron to be there at 8 am &
to return to Wizernes today.
Send machine gun & spare to station to be
handed over to Ordnance Officer -
Went to St Omer this morning -
Give out orders for Parade tomorrow at
8.15 am - 53 & 1 to be at Billets at 7.30 am
Will have to tow the Daimler No 1910 -
four wheels not yet arrived -
Paulmier goes to Vieun Berguin to try & arrange
billets -

10th March Wednesday - Vieux Berquin
Orderly officer Lieut Rubury.

Park parades at 8.15am - Everything is left
clean - Drive off at 8.30am Daimler
car has to be towed. Arrive at Vieux Berquin
11 am. Roads in fair condition. One lorry detailed
for RE left at 7.30am & will not be in till
tomorrow - Orders received to stand bye as we
may move at any hour. Billets very scattered.
Recommend Burltin for Temp Capt & other 2 Lieuts
for T. Lieuts. Send in maps not required to
General Staff office & to do see R.K.G.
at 2 P.M & have a long talk re returns etc.

Am.n Column require 32,000 rounds s.a.a.
& 5,100 rounds revolver am.n
List of maps returned see Cap/137.

10.30 P.M. Wire comes in for RE stores to be
drawn from Strazeele & handed over at 7am
to Brigades at Vieux-Berquin.
Detail Lt Burltin & give instruction that
lorry is to be at Strazeele Station at
6 am
Obtain some (2 galls) Castor oil from
Flying Corps for clutch leather.

11

11th March Thursday Nieuw Buzguin –
Orderly Officer Lieut Anderson.
No parade at 9.30 am men to clean up
round Park & to build incinerator.
8 am A.a & D.M.G. & Col Ellyatt arrived & said
that no lorry had turned up yet at Nieuwe
Buzguin. At 8.30am Buxton arrives
having delivered the stores to 4th Brigade
& had missed the A.a & D.M.G.
Following lorries require letgroing –
Daimler 5717 – Halley – 3341 – 5324
5741 – 3638 – The type press at Stiogude
can not do them until Saturday –
Wire to M.T.adv. Base to send all stores
etc to Cavalry Corps Supply Railhead –
Water Jacket cover received from Base
also Amac Carburetter for Douglas
Motor Bicycle –

Lt. Lothwaltz R.F.a to go to 2nd Cav Div
as soon as his successor arrives –

2nd Field squadron require 6000 S.A.a
& borrow 10 galls petrol.

Have lamps painted to prevent rays
dazzling approaching drivers – glass from
12 to 3 o'clock. reflector 6 to 9 o'clock

12th March Friday. View Burgers
Orderly Officer Lt Nisbet —
Send schedule No1 for March to Supply
Officer. V.C. ASC inspects my register
of vehicles. No comments. M.T. Base
wire that under instructions received from
DofT my stores have to be sent to GHQ. I
write to V.C. ASC for necessary authority
to have mine sent to Cavalry Corps Supply
Railhead. Send in Sunday strength at
B213 is to be compiled up to & including
Friday night rendered on Saturday.
2nd Lieut W.A. Mallows arrives in place of
2nd Lieut Gothwal 15 RFA. VC ASC to
inspect park at 9.30 am tomorrow. Three
lorries to be attached to Park with SAA for
Infantry & Bayode alta: to Division.
Go with P.R.O. to see ao of SoT.
4000 SAA issued to 2nd Field Squadron
RE. 96 rounds Revolver Amn. R.A.M.C.

13th March Saturday Vieux Arquin -
Orderly Officer Lt. Burlton -
Parade at 9.30 am for inspection of O.C
ASC 2nd Cav Div. everything appeared to be
very satisfactory - Furseon sent in a
report - sent states to a a + o.m.b accts &c
also to O/C ASC Records.
Lieut Burlton to go to the Supply Column -
Orders for Lt. Rothwell is not to proceed at present
to 2nd Indian Cavalry but to stand fast -
reported arrival of 2nd Lieut Mallows -
Furseon is to return to old billets round Vieux
-Arquin - Three lorries arrive Hallford Nos.
8869 - 8864 - 8845 - for 269 Coy ASC
Tool cases + spare tools arrive from
A.O.D. Vauxhall car requires overhaul
but at present it is the only car that is
reliable - It has not been touched since
the beginning of the war & has stood very
well indeed - Daimler cars are useless
the gears are always going, although
driven carefully - Workshops make
spare radius rods as three have
gone without any special reason -

14th March Sunday Vieux Berguin_

Orderly Officer 2" Rubury.

Report the departure of 2/Lt Hurllin who went to the Supply Column for duty today.

Church Parade at 12 mid day.

310 Fuzes drawn from Railhead for Warickshire R.H.A. in place of unserviceable fuzes in 13pr. In future the shells are to be returned to Railhead & have the fuzes taken out.

2nd Lieut W J Luck R F A arrived for duty at the Park report his arrival to the Div: & state that we have now got two Gunner officers. Send one lorry to C.A.S.C. for Coal. I only send lorries when all my Spares are running.

The coal lorry returns at 8 P.M. having broken a spring_front.

Church Parade at 12 mid day.
Amm'n return sent in.
Nominal roll of company sent to
O/c Records, 3rd Echelon.

15th March Monday. Vieux Berquin
Orderly Officer Lieut Anderson.

2nd Field Squadron require one lorry at 8.30am for stores from St Omer.

2'Lieut R L Gottwaltz R F A leaves for 2nd Indian Cavalry Division.

Returned 30 maps to G.S. asked if my full issue could be increased from 5 to 8 –
I have to get my maps from CRA. Issue has been increased to 8.

Major Leland came round to inspect Park. He was very satisfied with conditions of the lorries. Several small things. One seem to viz. Petrol account. Workshop book to have more detail. Separate set of books to be kept for ordering M.T. Stores. Also these will be kept separate. He promised to see about changing the place where my M.T. Stores are sent to viz St Omer. Also if any one has devised any means of strengthening ladies rods on Halleys.

Workshop Store lorry not satisfactory – 5341 to be repainted.

4 Head lamps arrive from M T Depot.

Tyres for Halley 5341 apparently can't be done at Hazebrouck but can't understand this letter must send an officer over to see about it.

16th March Tuesday. Vieux Berquin
Orderly officer Lieut Mabert —

Issue instructions for the up keep of
workshop books. Daily book to be kept
by M.S.M. Lorry book to be kept by o/c
workshops showing time + material
expended on each repair to each
lorry. Start petrol book — Anderson
goes to Hazebrouck re tyres — Write to M.T.
600 Base cancelling all previous demands
+ start afresh — Send in demand to G.H.Q.
to be sent down by the motor cyclist —
Parades as usual.
Receive 8 maps Hazebrouck 5A in
addition to set laid down.

Section officers to keep daily repair book
of work done in sections showing time &
material used + man working on it.
The daily work books will be entered
up into Workshops officer's repair book
+ record of vehicles once a week &
brought to O.C. Park for inspection

17

17th March Wednesday Oium Belgium
Orderly officer Lt Rubury.
One lorry bbe at Major Johnson's billet at
8.30am for R.E. Stores.
Recieve following maps from oc 2 C.S auxy Column
St Omer - 2 - Arras 7 - Ostend - 5. Ghent 4 -
Antwerp. 3 -
Start a separate book of work for my
demands on adv. M.T. Base.

Lorry sent to St Omer to draw M.T. Stores &
to pick up wheels retyred for Halley No 57241
at Hazebrouck on its return journey.

Issue 23000 rounds saa to Auxy
Column + one rocking bar.

Drills as usual.

Recieve maps from G.S and now I
am surplus those sent by Auxy Column
as above -

Two Halley wheels returned retyred.
The following stores recieved. 1 Halley
front axle complete, 1 Steering Rod
link, rod + arms. 4 Covers 820 x 120.
2 Covers 880 x 120. 7 Covers 26 x 2¼

18th March Thursday Views Bugle
Orderly Officer Lieut Anderson.

Orders received for 2Lieut Luck R.F.A. to
proceed to 3rd Cav Div Am'n Park.

Swage block & stand returned too Have
yesterday. The block did not fit into the stand
I wired 16-3 for new stand. The Block was
returned in error - returned by empty supply
train. 4 outer covers for cars & ✗ ✗ two for
motor cycles. unserviceable.

Issue 30000 S.a.a to 2" D.G to replace
unserviceable. Also 2100 rounds revolver
to 2nd D.G. ammunition Am'n Column &
582 rounds to 2" D.G.

A.D of S.O T came round to inspect at
3 P.M. Drills as usual.

Draw 600 rounds revolver from Railhead.

19th March Friday Vieux Berquin

Orderly Officer Dr Nisbet –

Draw picks & shovels from R.E. Park for
4th & 3rd Brigades –

24000 S.a.a. for 12th Lancers –

Make out schedule for week & send it to
Div. Troops Supply officer –

From the 19th (today) inclusive the supply for 13 pr
guns is limited to two rounds per gun per day
running account to be kept – no overdrawals
will be allowed – G.S.O.

Major Selands report on the Park received –
Points to be observed. Store lorry to be improved
with solid sides & wooden roof –
Repair book to be more exhaustive as regards
information given viz time & material used –

Col Gillson joins 3rd Cav Div. as C.R.A. –

All interpreters to wear a brassard, red &
white, whilst on top. Mons. Paulinier is to
be No. 18. marked outside I. C.a inside
C.a. 18. Mons. Paulinier to report to Capt.
Fayelle tomorrow morning –

20th March Saturday Vieux Berquin

Orderly officer Lieut Rubney.

Return sent to a.d. S+T. Cav Corps —

Small arms amm[unitio]n return to be sent in tomorrow at 12 mid-day.

I have to build a store lorry authority —
A D S+T. 227/15 of 18-3-15 — Q.L. 2323 —
a.s.c. H[ea]d q[uarter]rs. 162 —
A of T. 541 — Spare drivers increased to 50% — Bringing my total up to —
Rank & file 99. Total 122 —

Nisbet goes to St Omer to purchase wood screws etc & to arrange for wood at Hazebrouck

Return sent to a.s.c. Records & R.A. records.

Drills as usual.

21st March. Sunday.   21
                        Vieux Berquin
Orderly officer Lieut Anderson.

The second gear box Lorry 5346 found to
have a pin in reverse gear gone —
Fresh AB 213 sent in to Division with
amt Return showing S.A.A. 792 000 rounds.
+ 10 rounds per A.S.C. + 20 rounds per
R.F.A. See Col Longmore re Anderson.
Papers sent to A.D.S.+T.

Send Lorry to 2d Field Squadron to draw
bombs — a letter by D.R.L.S. from records
asking for names of men to go home — NCOs
surplus to establishment.

Send in name Pte M.S.M. Hardy.

Don't understand the way provisional ranks
are run — Not quite clear if I can promote
provisional ranks to complete establishment
+ if those ranks get pay or not.

No church Parade.

22nd March Monday.

Orderly Officer 2d Lieut. Nisbet –

Vauxhall Car sent into shops for general overhaul. In very bad condition.

Return 8 copies St Omer map to G.S.

Wire for gear wheels for lorry 5726.

Issue 3 boxes Revolver Amn.

Stores arrive at St Omer – A lot of complaints in the letters about food – Take disciplinary action.

Take Toomey off the Vauxhall & put on Lovick.

Issue 3 boxes Very's pistol cartridges to 20th Hussars.

Parades as usual.

Discover by trials that the best way for the man in rear of a lorry to signal to the driver is to have a small bicycle bell fitted up near driver with a string on it – or boden wire. Trouble will be to obtain the bells. Ask O.O. for necessary authority to purchase.

23rd March Tuesday. Vieux Bequin

Orderly officer Lieut Rubury.

Issue. 19000 saa
828 rnds revolver } Amn Coln.

Also. Springs firing gear 2.
" pinch hooks — 1.
" traversing lever — 2
" Sear firing — 1.

Send Lt= Orr for spares.

Draw 4000 francs from Paymaster.

Pay out to A.S.C. + R.A.M.C.

More stores received from M.T. Base. at St Omer

Purchase wood for workshop Lorry. Have
5341 painted. Drills as usual.

Receive Schedule No 2. from Div Troops S.O.

Apply to R.C. A.S.C. to send Daimler Car
to Paris as no jeans are available at
Adv. M.T. Base. Also to put the back axle
of 961 Daimler into 1910. as 1910 is
the better Car.

24th March Wednesday

Report to be sent in to A.D.S.T. on the new pattern links for the Crossley - Beverey non skids - They have not been received yet.

Orderly officer Lt. Anderson.

Draw 40000 rounds S.A.A from Railhead.

Receive a water cart from A.O.D. The question is to fix it. The Tank is round. +if put on a lorry the lorry may not be able to get near enough to the stream. If towed behind. How long will it last water tight?

Draw 1000 francs from Paymaster. & Pay out the R.E.a

Receive secret letter re Enemys Air Ships which I communicate to officers & then destroy. Am asked for a lorry at 9.30 P.M. to tow out another lorry which has got ditched at Lee-Bois.

R. A.S.C o/c D gives me verbal permission to send one lorry down to Rouen for spare parts.

25th March Thursday
Vieux Berquin
Orderly officer Lt Nisbet.

Secret Letter A.G. C/B/19 received & acknowledged
98 000 rounds S.a.a. required by Am[?]
Column. the same amount is drawn.
Report b.o.c. a.s.c. men who have been promoted
in the Shops. Prepare indent for Rubney.
If 2cm rations are used report is to be made
to Supply officer.

~~Two prisoners for drunk~~
2nd Lieut Mallow goes to England on leave
till 3rd April.

26th March 1915. Friday.
Vieux Berquin
Orderly officer Lt Anderson.
Lorry left for Rouen 6-15 am.
Send in Schedule for the week to
2nd Troops Supply officer.
Five men for office. Pte Burchett for
Court Martial. Pte Toomey 21 days &
Pte Edwards 21 days. Pte G. White
7 days. Drunk & creating disturbance
etc. Pte Lawson case dismissed.
Issue one box S.A.A. to North Mid. Brigade
The following stores arrive. Sprocket Shafts for
G. Type Hallry. Front axle complete for
B. Type axle. 7 Covers 26 + 2¼. This latter
is evidently duplicated. Wire to
M.T. Depot to cancel gears for Daimler
Car No. 1910. permission being granted
to send it to Paris.
Lt Rubury goes to Rouen in charge of
Lorry.
Cancelled parade at 2.0 pm. as Park is playing
R.A.M.C. at football.

27th March Saturday.   27

                          Vann-Buquin
Orderly Officer L: Nisbet.

Wire to D.A.T. ASD Depot to cancel from the
list Rubery is taking down parts received
yesterday.

Back axle of Daimler Car No 961 taken
out & put into Car No 1910. as the latter
car is the better of the two.

Send in Summary of evidence against   MS/1280
Bushett. Draw + issue to Oxford Hussars.

   25 Bombs + detonators No 8.
    8 Fathoms Fuse Safety No. 9.
    2 lbs Gutting common
    2 Boxes matches safety.

Make out slates for 2-car Div. a&s s+t. o/c
     Revd. also at B 20 6g.
Lieut Anderson goes to a & s off s+t.

Issue 10000 rounds S.a.a. to 12th Lancers.

Authority to send Daimler Car No 961 to Paris
is a&s s+t 42/34. o.c. a.s.c. 178.

28th March — Sunday

Send in certificate re cameras to OC & ORMC. Vieux Berquin
O.L. 2603.

Ammunition return.
Orderly officer Lt Anderson.

Church Parade 9 am under orderly officer.
Pt Benchett drunk on 8 am working Parade
5000 S.A.A. to Amn Column.
With-draw all iron rations from men.
Spare jear wheels sent for Halley Lorry

29th March Monday
                                    Vieux Berquin -
Orderly officer Lt Nisbet.
Car Darkener No. 961 sent to Railhead
for dispatch to Paris.
Send lorry to collect wood for posts for
Head Qrs. Send lorry to Thiezule R E
Park Railhead for sandbags gun cotton
etc for units of 2nd Cav Div.
Issue 16000 rounds SAA to Royal
Scots 21st Brigade 7th Div - as they
could not find their Park -
Issue to units - receipts filed.
Gear wheels arrive for Halley's starter motors.
Fitted a B type front axle & steering to an
old type 3 ton Halley - Had to make new
brushes but otherwise very satisfactory.
Only fault in Vauxhall. gears slightly
worn. one exhaust valve badly burnt
The engine was dirty. But in very good
condition considering it has run
continuously since 15th August.

30th March Tuesday

Vieux Berquin

Report to be sent to O.C. asc re complaints from officers re claims sent to Paymaster.

Report to A.D. of S+T details of electric lighting sets in mobile workshops — Engine makers name + no of cylinders — Dynamo makers name.

Send Imprest Account to Paymaster. Balance in hand 746-15 francs.

Draw 30000 S.A.A. from Railhead - 410 boxes of revolver = 2760 rounds.

Draw 150 very pistol cartridges & issue to 20 Hussars. Parades as usual.

9 P.M. Lorry returns from Rouen having obtained most of the stores.

Orderly officer Lieut Anderson.

M.T. Stores now arrive at Supply Railhead for Cavalry Corps instead of at G.H.Q. Have to indent on A.D. of S+T for new Car instead of O.C. asc.

31st March Wednesday   31

                    Dinan Bruguier
Orderly Officer Lieut Nisbet -
Return of officers, motor cars & strength
per unit - due -
Write to O/C Rd. Records re proper carrying
pay of Three gunners. Indent on A of FST
for new car -
Return of motor cycles sent in to C
A.S.C
   Issue 600 rounds revolver &
   3000 S.A.A   to 20th Hussars -
Pte Burchett warned for Court Martial
at 6.P.M - for 10am next day - Lieut
Anderson warned to attend as witness
also write to M.O i/c H.P trash for Staff
Q.M.S. Davies to attend -
Obtain permission for Lieuts Rubury
& Nisbet to attend under instruction -

            G.E. Goldsmith Capt
                    A.S.C
        O.C. 2nd Cav Div. Amm Park.

1 4/15 -

2nd Aus. Div. Amm'n Park.

Vol VI - 30.4.15

32

1st April Thursday
Orderly officer Lieut Rubury. Vice Kinnier. Drill
parade at 8 a.m. wished off at
9.30 a.m. Send Diary to F. the Base.
Letter from Paymaster. Acg. Roll 9-15 d/
4-3-15, for 4,615. Roll 9 to 12.10 7/6
+ not 13.10 francs.
Issue to 20th Hussars. 24000 S.a.a. &
552 rounds Revolver.
Court martial on Pte Burchett 10 a.m.
Major Cook D.S.O 20th Hussars president.
Lieut Anderson goes to St Omer for new
Car. Vauxhall No   arrives.
13 men arrived last night from Rouen
one Blacksmith + 12 drivers.

2nd April Friday
Orderly Officer Lt. Anderson. Vieux Berquin
Ordered behind the three Halfords
back to the North Midland Div with their
ammunition. Report arrival of Vauxhall
Send in schedule for week —
Issue 7000 SAA 6th DG
" 4000 SAA 2nd DG
5000 SAA 12th Lancers.
600 rounds revolver 6th DG.
Draw from Railhead — 34000 SAA
Issue 50 sand bags to 5th Lancers
50 " " " 4th Hussars.

3rd April Saturday
                    Quin bequin

Orderly Officer Lt Nisbet —

Detail one lorry for Coal.

Send in returns for week.

B 243 sent in last week to O/c Records
not signed + no heading — Office copy
sent in by mistake —

A Sof S & T wired for return of cars — Return
already sent to oc. ASC 0th div —

147 Coy R.E mining coy belonging to 1st
Army want to borrow 4 3 Ton Jacks —
I have 3 spare in workshops as well + two
heavy jacks so say I can lend them —

4th April Sunday.
Treux Buquin
Orderly Officer 2nd Rubury.

New Censor Stamp No 333 received old
one No 1536 destroyed by me.
Send lorry for wood. Send in billet
return under new scheme. 5 officers
1 hulipit & 47 other ranks.

All returns for O/C Records have to be
sent by despatch rider letter post.

2nd Mallows returns from leave.

In future returns of motor cars is to be sent
direct to AD & SS & T. Cavalry Corps.

Promulgate sentence of Pte C. Burchett 1/3
6 months Imp H.L. for (1) disobedience of
orders (2) drunk on parade at 8 am

36

5th April Monday.
Orderly Officer Lt. Anderson. Vieux Berquin

Pte Burchell C handed over to the R.T.O Steenbecque
100 suits dungaree arrive from aod
they have been on order for months.
Very wet no parades.
Douglas workshop engine wire for spare parts.
Exchange oblong boxes. of S.A.A 850 for
square boxes containing 1000 with 5th
Cav Brigade as square boxes don't
fit very well on pack animals.

6th April Tuesday
Vieux Berquin

Orderly Officer Lt Nisbet.

Have to send in a daily Casualty Report to AA & QMG

Complaint about the dangerous way detonators are issued case in point on the 1st April Unit 5th Cav Brigade Scots Greys drew from R.E Park direct.

Receive stationary. Army Act. Field Service Regs. & C.B.C. etc.

38

7th April Wednesday
Vieux Berquin
Orderly officer Lt Rubury.
Receive orders from AA & QMG. & hand
over 288 rounds 13pr to St Venant
Am[munition] Railhead. Draw Detonators & gun-
cotton etc & issue to 4th Cav. Brigade.
ADofS&T require return showing amount
of petrol etc used when standing to &
when we are moving.

8th April Thursday
Vieux Berquin.

Orderly officer Lt Anderson.

Draw 5000 francs from Field Cashier
+ 125 frs for personal use.
Send in Field & Light & Lodging claims —

R.E. Pack will not issue with a demand
countersigned by A.A. & Q.M.G. for 2nd Field Squadron

Third speed wheel in gear box on lay
shaft arrives. I have put back the old one
& hold this as spare.

9th April Friday.
                    Vieux Bergaim
Orderly officer Lieut Nisbet.

Send in feeding strength 121. and schedule
for supplies purchased during the week
No 2 for April Acc:—

Send in return re amount of petrol + oil
likely to be required when at rest &
when on the move.

Pay out to the Park. Most of the gunners
are in debt.

10th April Saturday.
                    Vieux Berquin

Orderly Officer Lieut Rubury —
Make out States etc — Send the copy of
B 213 to O/C Records by despatch rider
letter service —
Have no Army Form A.10. to send to Base
re Burchett Court Martial.
Indent on Stationery office for some —

11th April Sunday
Vieux Berquin

Orderly officer Lieut Anderson –
Church Parade 11-15 am for C of E &
10 am for R.C
No route march today –
Go down to see the German trenches taken
at Neuf Chappel –
Dig out the clay patches in the square
& put down rubble –

12th April Sunday
Vieux Berquin

Orderly Officer Lieut Nisbet –

Went to St Omer to try to buy some gun-
metal but could not get any.
Orders came in to collect 6 mortars from
3rd & 4th Brigades & then to draw 600
rounds bomb am'n & take up to Ypres.
Anderson went in charge & returned at 10 P.M.
Reported to AA & QMG.
Ordered to have two batteries ready to move
as Warwick shire RHA are being transferred
to 1st Cav Div.

13th April Tuesday
Vieux Burquin

Orderly officer Lieut Rubury.
See D.O. & get him to wire for gun metal as
it is urgently required. Certain a.o.t
stores arrive. At 3 P.M. orders came in to
hand over lorries to 1st Cav div. Lt
Rubury in charge. 1st C. & a P. not in place
notified but found eventually at Ebblinghen
new store lorry completed.
Lorry that went to Ypres broke front spring.
Have pow-pow with officers about springs.
result issue orders that all springs are to
be taken down washed in paraffin & oiled.

45

14th April Wednesday.
         Vieux Berquin

Orderly officer Lieut Anderson.

22 Waist coats fur sent down to Railhead
for despatch to Paris.

Draw 1000 Francs Imprest Acc.

Report departure of 2 Daimlers.

All AoD incidents previous to 1-2-15 are
cancelled.

Start painting four lorries.

General clean up round park. Make
better arrangements as regards refuse, but
civilian population come & dump by
the Park.

46

15th April Thursday
Orderly officer Lieut Mabel - Meure Burquin

Send in return of motor cars to a.a.a.f.f. + T. -
Drew 11 Mortars from St Venant & issued
2 to 5th Brigade. 4 to 3rd Brigade &
5 to 4th Brigade -
Toomey & Edwards finish their Field
punishment -
Go to Vieille Chappel to 34th Pioneers - see
Armstrong. Parades as usual. Weather
fine.

16th April Friday. Vieux Berquin

Orderly officer Lieut Rubury.
Make out & send in Schedule for the
week.
Feeding strength return.
Draw & issue 180 sandbags to 5th Lancers
Spare gun parts practically complete.

48

17th April Saturday
                    Vieux Berquin
Orderly officer Lieut Anderson.
Make out weekly returns & take a/B 213
b a d of 8 r t.
Send return to O/C R.A. Records re casualties
in R.A. — Send to Records a/B 103 for
the men asked for.
Divisional Horse Show in afternoon.

18th April Sunday
Vieux Burquin

Orderly officer Lieut Nisbet.

No Church Parade for CofE. RC's at 11-15.

Lorry No. 3341 went yesterday to Hazebrouck to be retyred in front. It was done at Steenvoorde on the 14th March & only run about 400 miles & the rubber had perished

19th April Monday
Vieux Berquin

Orderly Officer Lieut Rubury.

Two armoured car attached to Division with 3 pounders - no amm.t arrived and no notification at present about drawing same. Make arrangements with R.A.M.C. for hot baths for the men & cleaning of blankets & clothing.

No wood to be obtained in Hazebrouck for sides of lorries etc.

Parades during last week as usual.

Indent for 122 Iron Rations Grocery - most of them are broken & spoilt. 100 were issued time in November 1914

20th April Tuesday. Vieux Berquin

Orderly Officer Lieut Anderson.
Eight men to go each hour from 10 a.m.
for hot baths.
Send spare lamps electric to Base.
Issue 2000 Rounds S.a.a. to Supply
Column. Check a/B 122.
No Gun - metal to be had from Dishamne
Send Nisbet to hieuville to try & purchase
wood to make sides & tail board for
lorry. Wood available in two days.
Workshops at last ahead of work.
Motor cycles in for overhaul.

21st April Wednesday
Vieux Berquin
Orderly officer Lieut Nisbet.
No drill parade 7 a.m. on account
of rain -
Draw 5000 francs from Field Cashier
Route march at 2. P.M.
Draw 122 Iron Grocery Rations -
The whole of the bedding & clothes
of the men of Park fumigated - &
all men have hot bath.

53

22nd April Thursday
Vieux Burquin

Orderly Officer M.S.M. Hardy.

Lt Nisbet goes to Hinville & one to try &
purchase wood & Wrought Iron.

I go with Perry Kerr Gore to Pont Riquel
to look at roads for Supply Column & Park
as guns are being lent to 7th Divisn.

Pay out the Company.

P/o Corpl Hornby goes to ? for his teeth &
is reverted to rank of Pte

23ʳᵈ April Friday
Vieux Berquin

Orderly officer Lieut Rubury.

Orders received for Division to concentrate.

I am a member of Court Martial at 10 am at "B" Echelon field Ambulance.

Division moves off at 1. P.M. Head Quarters at ~~B~~ BOESchepe.

Sent in Schedule for week & feeding strength to S.O. Div. Troops.

Orders for the Park to remain in billets at present.

Light sect of Am⁺ Coln. to X roads ½ mile N.E of FLETRE

Send P⁺ White as cycle orderly H.Q.C.

24th April Saturday.
Nieu. Berquin

Orderly officer Lieut Anderson.
Make out & send in states a/f/b 213.
etc. Advance sect of Am[mn]t Column
Light sect moves to BOESCHEPE.
No amm[n]t required.
Stats sent b.a.b. of S&T.
Two wheelers lent to Supply Column
who are short of artificers.
Roads round Nieu Berquin going North
blocks with troops.
Pte Hornby discharged from H.P. promoted
Cpl.

25th April. Sunday.
Vieux Bergum

Orderly officer Lieut Nisbet —
Send to Am.t Column at 8. am
no am.t required —
Send following A/B 122 — Williams, Barnsdale
Dyson & Hewitt to Base men adm to H —
Ammunition Return sent in —
no church parade —
Route march 2 pm to 4 —

26th April Monday.
from Busquim to Fletre
Orderly officer. M.S.M. Hardy. J.
Sent in return to A&QMG re type
of lorries. & number of passengers required
by A.S.C.
Ordered to send up 2000 sand bags to
Head Quarters.
Orders to move to Fletre at 11.30 am
moved at 12.30 P.M. via Castre.
Send Anderson to reconitre roads to
Boesechepe — Water cart not a success
trailing — Certain parts shake to pieces —
Have to fill up about 1½ miles away.
Report to DAQ & QMG
Ant-i Column reports guns in action —

27th April Tuesday "FLETRE"
Orderly officer Lt. Rubury.

7.30 am 612 rounds 13pr required
Send Lt Rubury. Send Lt Anderson
8.30 to Vieux-Berquin. I inspect
Lorries with workshop officer.

9.15 am. another 1000 rounds 13pr
required send Lt Nisbet with 1200 Rows.
at 9.30. am. Total number of rounds
issued 1012. ~~tax~~ 13pr.

1.P.M. requisition for 10,000 sandbags +1500
Very flares. Draw from Strazeele. can
only get 9 boxes of 120 flares. 1000 x 13pr.
Lorry returns at 10.30 P.M. having issued
beyond Ypres.

7.30 P.M. Column ask for 440 rounds
13pr early tomorrow morning.

Interpreter of 69 Bg. a.s.c. asks if he can
confine a man in my guard room
at 10.30 P.M. to be handed over to French
Authorities next day. Suspicious
Character. Cpl Fergusson N.C.O. i/c Guard

28th April Wednesday
Hetre.
At midnight Column asks for another
900 rounds 13pr to be sent up daily.
Five lorries under Lieut Anderson
leaves at 7.30 am. Prisoner handed over
to French guard. H.Qrs moved to point
36 near junction of 5 roads 2½ miles S.W of
VLAMERTINGHE. Send orderly to Vieux-
Berquin for orders.
Column take 1208 rounds. Draw there at
1 PM from Steenvoorde.

Lorry No   cast an inside rear tyre
sent to Steenvoorde at 3 P.M. returns at 9 P.M.
at 3.30 R.E. field Squadron requires one
lorry to report at 6 P.M. at Camp.
returned at 3. am having had to do two
journeys to beyond Ypres.

Column require 604 rounds 13pr.
at 10am tomorrow orderly arrived at
10 P.M.

60

29th April Thursday
7 L'ête
Orderly officer Lieut Nisbet —
Rubury takes up 604 rounds to Column
at 9 a.m. Cycle orderly to Neun-Berquin
Receive 17 passes for May & June —
Two lorries for 2d Field Squadron required
at 5. P.M —
Motor Cyclist lent to Amn Column to keep up communication
between Park & Column taken by C.R.a
A lot of empty shell cases returned —
Springs fitted to water-cart & rubber connection
put in on the pump. The whole thing is too
rigid & even now I don't think it will
stand the shaking behind the lorries —

30th April Friday Flêtre.

Orderly officer R.S.M. Hardy.

Only one lorry returned at 3 am from Ypres the other lorry met with an accident & hit a tree. Break down lorry starts at 9.30 am. I see A.A. & Q.M.G. about my cycle orderly. & White is returned to Column.

Lorry smashed up one kilo. West of Ypres Chassis badly bent has to be towed back. Lorry gets back at 6 P.M.

One Lorry wanted by 2nd Field Squadron at 5 P.M. — returns at 1 am.

108 rounds 13pr sent up to Column at 9 am. Draw from Hazebrouck at 2 PM.

One 13pr damaged belonging to "J" Battery returned to Am.n Railhead.

With draw all old passes & hand out new.

G. L. Goldsmith Capt
A.S.C.
2/5/15. O.C. 2 Cav Div Am. t Park

131/5607

a2
a56

2nd Cavalry Division

2nd Cav: Div: Ammn Park.

Vol XII May 1915

D. A. G.
    3rd Echelon Base

Herewith diary for May.

2nd Cav. Div. Ammn. Park.

A. R. Goldsmith Capt
A.S.C.
O.C. 2 Cav Div Ammn Park.

62

12th May — Saturday   Hesdin —
    Orderly Officer Lieut Rubury.

Send in cycle orderly to St Omer to find out if they can take in Lorry Halley No 5348 for repairs
848 rounds sent up to Amn Column at 9. am
Lorry 5348 sent into St Omer.
Returns etc for end of month & week sent in for all, at S+T, S ref T & so adM.G &
O/C Records.

at 7. P.M. the Column asks for 200 rounds 13 pr. sent up lorry returned at 10.30 P.M.
Lorry towing 5348 to St Omer returns at 10.30 P.M. Pte Wright & Murphy go in with lorry.
at 2. P.M. drew 848 rounds 18 pr from Railhead

63

2nd May – Sunday. FLETRE.

Ord'ly officer Lieut Anderson.

Draw 200 rounds 13pr from Railhead 9am.

Send in Diary for April to BAC 3rd Echelon.

Send in O.1838 for Pte Wiles 14/- a week from 13-2-15 & for Pte Pritchard 11/- per day from 1-4-15

Report billets in Fletre. Officers 5. Sub 1. men with beds 8. 26 shelter 1 office.

No ammunition required. Send up lorry to column to bring in empty shell cases & open boxes of SAA. also limber damaged of "E" Bty. "B" Echelon to move tomorrow at 9am from Vieux Berquin. DAD & Mi G writes to tell me not to report my billets now to Maire.

3rd May. Monday   **64**
                   FLETRE

Send Certificat re motor bicycles surplus
to establishment — D.O.C. asc

Head Qrs move to Esquelbecq —

Orders received to send two lorries
13 pr to IV. Corps am⁺ Park at Hazebrouck
& to move Park to Esquelbecq on the 4th

Orderly officer Lieut Nisbet.

Ordered to pick Pte Crosley & motor cycle
at Caestre tomorrow morning —

4th May Tuesday.

Fletre to Zegers Cappel

Move at 8 a.m. I send 5 lorries 13 pr to IV Corps + 1 spare gun pack lorry - arrive at Esquelbecq at 10.30 a.m. All the billets taken. Receive a wire to send to G.H.Q. for another lorry. See A.A.&Q.M.G. & get permission to billet at Zegers Cappel 2 miles West of Esquelbecq. Lorry Halley No 7937 arrives at 2 P.M. from St Omer. Supply Railhead Steenbecque.

Orderly Officer ~~Lieut Rodway~~.
                              M.S.M. Hardy.

66

5th May Wednesday.
                    Zeggers Cappel.
Orderly officer Lieut Rubury.
General clean up & over haul of lorries.
Send in report on billets.
Orders received to stand by for move.
Tyres on water Cart require to be shortened
& shrunk on. Fix up circle to do this.
Water Cart travelled very well on the
Springs & rubber connection on pump.
Pte Crossley rejoins the H.Qrs but leaves
his bicycle. Requires several slight
repairs & new induction pipe. Obtain
a new induction pipe from Hazebrouck.

6th May Thursday
                    Zegers Coppel.
Orderly officer Lieut Anderson.
Column require 42 ovo SAA 41 bom
revolver Amn. No revolver in Pack send
Rubney to Thorgule for 4 boxes.
Send Car to Armoured Cars to go to Drunkite
(10miles) for spares.
Supply Railhead Steenbecque — one
bm MT Stores at Railhead.
CRA wants a motor cyclist whilst
Batteries are detached from Division. I
lend one on the understanding that
he is returned to Amn Column when
the batteries rejoin.

68

7th May Friday. Zegers Cappel
orderly officer to Nisbet. Vieux Berquin
Send in schedule for week. Last week's
not yet received from Supply officer —
Send in Ration return.
Pte Wheeling absent off his guard at
9.30 P.M last night. Evidence shows
he was taken short.
Orders received that Division moves this
afternoon to Vieux. Berquin Detail
orders to be issued later.
Issue 1 box Revolver amn to Column.
At 1. P.M. receive orders to move to Vieux —
Berquin via Cassel. Caestre. Move off
at 2-30 P.M. Troops not clear so have
to wait 1½ hours on road. Arrive at
7. P.M.

8th May. Saturday. River Bugia [?]

Orderly officer M.S.M Hardy J.

Send in Relieving return. also weekly
state. Issue 10000 rounds S.A.A 15th Brigade
before 8.a.m. Draw Sand-bags & Shovels
at 7 a.m & Explosives for Div: & deliver
to units. Two lorries.

5. P.M. another lorry required for sandbags
deliveries + return at 7.30. P.M.

7.30 PM RE Field Squadron require one
big lorry to take bridging material to
trenches —

A.O.H & T not satisfied the way I have
shown the 18 men detached —

Orders received at 9.30 PM for Division
to concentrate at 5 am tomorrow.

Motor cycle Pte White damaged. Shops
work on it all day.

70

9th May. Sunday.
Orderly Officer Lieut Rubury. Vieux Berquin

Lorry sent to R.E Field Squadron returns
at 5 a.m.   Pte White's motor cycle
finished at 4 a.m the returns to
Ammⁿ Column — Send a motor cyclist
to CRA (Cpl Hornby) only to help them
out of a difficulty —

Send new AFB 213 to o/c ASC Records.
Ammⁿ Return to show total no of rounds.
Issue explosives etc to whole Divisi[on]

10th May. Monday. Vieux Berquin
Orderly officer Lieut Anderson.
Nisbet goes to St Omer to buy nuts & bolts.
Draw 6000 francs from Paymaster.
Pay out. Go through AB 64 to verify
& make out a new book nominal Roll.
One lorry to issue R.E. Park stores
to 3rd Cav Brigade — 3rd C Brigade
return two Mortars which are to be
kept on the park for the time being.
Issue 17000 rounds to Am.t Column.

11th May. Tuesday

Orderly officer Lieut Nisbet — Vieux Berquin

Lorry at 7.0 am to draw explosives
& to go round under A/O. W.O. to issue
explosives.

Lieut Nisbet goes to Merville to try to purchase
wood.

12th May Wednesday.
                    Vieux Berquin

Orderly officer M.S.M Hardy.
2nd Lieut J L. Pollard ASC. joins the Park.
Hand over a pair of CAV head lamps
to 2nd Cav Div Am'n Park. L/Cpl Cooper to
go to Supply Column.
Another lorry to go round with explosives
T.2 Lieut W F Nisbet sick. Not bad enough
to go to H.P.
Send a lorry to Neuville for wood cost
66.55 francs. To make a roof & side for
workshop lorry.
33,000 SAA issued to Am'n Column
& the same amount drawn from
Am'n Railhead.

74

13th May Thursday.
Orderly Officer Lieut Rubury.   Vieux-Berquin
T/Lieut R.L Anderson leaves the Park to
proceed to England for duty —
Report arrival of Lt Pollard & departure of Lt
Anderson, to O.C. A.S.C.

Collect mortars from units to be stored
at Head Quarters of Div —
Send imprest account away Balance
due to Paymaster on this account. 918·40 fr.
Orders received at 8.30 P.M. for Cavalry
to move remainder to stand by.

14th May Friday. Vieux Berquin
Orderly Officer 2 Lieut Pollock.
Draw 26000 SAA from Railhead to
Complete Park – make out schedule &
send it in.

Pte White returns from Heavy Echelon
& is sent to Light Echelon.

Cpl Hornby returns from C.R.A.

6.30 P.M. 5000 sand bags + 300 very
Pistols required. Tony leaves under
L/Cpl Turner returns from Maurestique
at 1. a.m.

Orders received for Lieut Pollard to go
to Supply Column & Capt Howard to
join the Park.

75

76

15th May Saturday -
Vieux - Berquin
Orderly officer M.S.M. Hartley -
Make out states B 213. + Cas returns -
Capt W.E.W. Howard joins the Park & 2nd Lieut
J.L. Pollard leaves -
See A.D.O.S. & T about P+M motor cycles -
Ask if both can be sent to the base or good
on the R.T.C. & bad one to base - No M.T
stores for P+M motor cycles at Base -
Draw Very flares & fuse from RE Park
Railhead & send up by Car to VLAMERTINGHE
CRA. complains about the communication
between the Heavy Echelon & the Park -
As these lorries are detached from me
& attached to another Corps it does not
concern me.

16th May Sunday
Vieux Berquin
Orderly officer Lieut Rubury —

Send M.S.M Hardy to St Omer at 7.30am to draw 1000# respirators & to take them up to Vlamertinghe. Report arrival of Capt W.E.W. Howard —

Send lorry to Head-Quarters Vlamertinghe — go & see CRA & explain that the lorries are attached to 4th AP & do not come under me at all. Then go to see a.a.d.M.G. who refers the matter to IV Corps. I suggest I send the whole of heavy section under my own officer to supply the guns & to be responsible for all communication —

17th May. Monday.
Vieux Berquin

Orderly Officer Lieut Nisbet –

One lorry required to be at 9th Field Squad at 5. P.M – Warn the D.A.D. & D.M.G. that they are working my spare lorries & I may in case of break. down have none available for R.E work. But Park does so little that there is not much chance of this happening – Go to Hazebrouck & see A.P.M as I hear that supplies are given away & get them to keep a watch on the shop.

50 Scoops required in the trenches none available any where so make some out of petrol tins –

Fill up vacancies in Corpl & L. Cpls.

Capt Howard takes up Detonators & fuze to Column for 20th Hussars –

78

18th May Tuesday.
Vieux Berquin
Orderly Officer M.S.M. Hardy —
Lorry leaves at 7.30am for Hazebrouck
the other lorry returned at 11 P.M. last night —
Report sent in that lorry has broken a
spring & will require oil & petrol —
Send up a car with new spring & get it
fitted. Warn N.CO. to go dead slow on
all roads round Ypres —
Lorry likely to be kept by Field Squadron

80

19th May. Wednesday
                    Vieux-Berquin

Orderly Officer Capt Howard -
Mallows went to Column.

100 rifle grenades asked for. sent up.
Send Nesbit to Poperinghe to buy spring steel
place was closed -
11.30am General Fagalt ordered me by telephone
to send 1200 rounds 13pr to 1st A.P. 1st Corps
at Dellins. Rubury delivered them returned
at 5.P.M no 13pr available to refill.
Drew 125" grenades double cylinder at
6.P.M. & sent them up to Vlamertinghe -
160 rounds 13pr with uncapped fuzes
sent by 3rd C.D.A.P. I sent them on
to 7th A.P. to be issued as soon as
possible -
Lorry sent yesterday to 3rd Field Squadron
to be kept by them for 3 or 4 days

20th May Thursday.
Vieux Berquin
Orderly officer Lieut Rusbury.

Mallows go to Column with bolts & nuts.
The 125 Double cylinder bombs returned. No anti
13 pr at Strazeele. Drew 1 box Very Flares —
No 13 pr arrived today at Strazeele —
Send up Very flares — Two boxes to Scots Greys
Go to Hazebrouck to see A.P.M. see Camp
Commandant & report to him that about 6 lbs
bacon was taken to Shop 31. Rue de ——
on the 19th inst. Pte Coomber saw the
bacon in the sack which was taken in —
Send up 100 loop hole plates —

21st May Friday.
                    from Buquin
Orderly Officer Lieut Nisbet —
No 13pr ammunition at Strazeele —
Coy QMS Elliott arrested in Hazebrouck for
disposing of bacon. Mallows goes to Ammunition
Column. Loop-hole plates taken to Corps
R.E Park which causes delay as no one
knows they are there — Cpl J/c Lorry was
told that that was the correct place for 2d
Field Squadron —

82

22" May. Saturday.

Vieux - Berquin -

Orderly Officer M.S.M. Hardy.

Remand Elliott for Court Martial & go & see
a.P.M Hazebrouck.

Lorry at 2 Field Squadron broken down
with spring. Officer reports load exceeds
4½ Tons. Send up another lorry & write to
A.A & Q.M.G. to give necessary orders for this
over loading to stop.

Monsieur Paulmier obtains a statement from
Mrs Renaut against Elliott.

23rd May Sunday.
Vieux-Berquin
Ordering Officer Capt Howard –
No 13 p Am E at Railhead – send in a
– Nil – return –
English Aeroplane brought down ½ mile away
by German Gun fire. Both men killed –
Send in Schedule of Supplies for the week
2nd Lieuts Rubury & Mabet promoted Lieuts –

84

24th May. Monday.
Vieux Berquin
Orderly officer Lieut Rubury
One lorry sent up to Reninghelst with 3 boxes
desiccators —
Change the six lorries on detachment &
send 6 that have not run much lately —
At 10. P.M. had to turn out a lorry to take
1000 rounds mortar Amn
12 mortars
60 lbs black powder
24 sprayers —
I had the mortars in the Park the bomb
Amn the only stuff available at
Railhead —
No 13 pr Amn available —

25th May Tuesday
                    Vieux-Berquin
Orderly officer Lieut Nisbet,
No. 13 pr aunt? at Railhead.
Draw 6000 francs from Field Cashier.
Head Quarters have kept the lorry which was
sent up last night for work.
Nisbet pays out for me.

26th May Wednesday. Vieux Bergier
Orderly officer M.S.M. Hardy.
No 13pr available —
Division to move on 31st to his Area
Park to be on the Argues Cassel road
just East of railway crossing —
G.O. of S+T arrives at 3P.M. to look
at Park & workshops.
M.S.M. Hardy made Permanent rank
Corps order 44 —

27th May - Thursday.
Vieux-Berquin

Orderly Officer Capt Howard -
Settle bill for wood - Sent Mallows trees
to get 13 pr - none available - goes to column
with rockets etc.

Send in fresh evidence & another charge
against Reso. Coy Q.M.S. Elliott -

Send Lt Nisbet & Mr Paulmier to look for
billets in new area -

28th May. Friday.
Vieux Berquin

Orderly Officer Lieut Rubury.

No. 13 for available.

Send in Schedule of Supplies purchased.

Elliott warned for Court Martial. Given summons. Capt Howard to be a member

Go to see OC ASC & lend him a car for billeting

29th May. Saturday

Nunn Bugui[?]

Orderly Officer Mr Nisbet,
Send in Returns. aB 213 A. etc
make out a list of returns required —
Court martial at 10 am on Coy QMS Elliott
Found Not Guilt on the charge of Fraud &
Guilty under Sect 40 —

30th May. Sunday   91

                                Vieux. Berquin
   Orderly Officer. M.S.M. Hardy.
Receive orders to move on 31st to Eblinghem
area. Pack to move at 7 a.m.
Send in Billeting returns
3 Lorries to go to Oxford Hussars to
carry tents & 1 for Head Quarters at
6 a.m 31st.
No.13 pr available.
Lorry from Am'n Column returns &
later on one from R.E. Field Squadron
returns.

92

31st May. Monday.
   Vieux Rucquin to Fort Rouge
Orderly officer Lieut Rubury.
Capt Goldsmith goes on leave 7.30am
Park moves at 7.am. Place cleaned
up etc. Arrive at Fort Rouge 9.am
Latrines etc dug.
No. 13 pr available.
7 men go on leave. sent by lorry
to St Omer at 7.30 P.M.
Car lent to 3rd Hussars to go to Boulogne
returns at 9.30 P.M.
Lorries from Oxford Hussars returns at
4.30 P.M.

     G.R. Goldsmith Capt
       A.S.C.
   O.C. 2 Cav Div Amm Park

2nd Cav. Division

2nd Cav: Div: Ammu: Park

WD VIII 1 — 30.6.15

121/5870

1st June. Tuesday.
                    Fort Rouge.

Orderly officer Lieut Nisbet.
Two lorries loaded with shovels + explosives
go to Steenbecque to off-load. at 10 a.m.
No. 13 pr amm? available_
1000 francs drawn from Field Cashier
for pay of men proceeding on leave_
The Batteries return to Division but the
lorries have not returned_
O.C. A.S.C. calls for return of officers
recommended for Temporary rank.
Hear unofficially that lorries (6) are
being used for R.E. work near St
Venant.

2ᵈ June Wednesday.
                    Fort Rouge.
M.S.M. Hardy. Orderly officer —
Draw 1000 Francs from Field Cashier —
One lorry for AOD for stores —
Lieut Rubury goes to see the attached
lorries which have moved towards St
Venant — Indent for respirators —
AOD lorry has to go to Sailly-sur-la
-Lys to 8ᵗʰ Division Ordnance Depot.

3rd June Thursday.
                    Fort Rouge.
Orderly Officer Lieut Rubury.
Lieut Nisbet goes on leave. Capt Goldsmith
returns from leave.

4th June Friday.
                    Fort Rouge.
Orderly officer M SM Hardy J
Send in Schedule for supplies to two
Troops S.O. also feeding strength.
O.C. A.S.C. inspects Park. no comments.

5th June Saturday.
Fort Rouge

Send in returns for week.
Show men on leave on AB 213 A.
Orderly officer ~~Lieut~~ Captain Howard.
Pte Dowsbrough drunk in workshop at 9 am.
Coy Q.M.S. Elliot H. reduced to the ranks & sentenced to 56 days No 1 Field Punishment. Promulgated by me at 8. am. Handed over to A.P.M. at 10 am.

6th June Sunday.
Fort Rouge.
Orderly officer Lieut Rubney.
R.A car to be sent to C.R.A as brigades
was billeted far apart, to be returned as
soon as div: moves —
Have bathing parade at 1.30 P.M. in the
Arques Canal — under orderly officer —
Send lorry to draw explosives for 16th Lancers
& Shovels & picks for 3rd Cav: Brigade —
Send in Am'n return 116 rounds 13 pr
only in Park instead of 2700 —
Billeting return sent in — After despatch
new return required giving names of
inhabitants etc. Send Paulmier to
Vieux Berquin to find out names.
D' Mallows can not get leave. His leave
to count as an A.S.C. officer in
the Park —

7th June Monday.
                    Fort Rouge –
Orderly officer M.S.M. Hardy.
Send 5000 SAA to 20th Hussars –
One lorry to St Omer AOD Stores.
— — — — Coal. OC. ASC
Issue 34200 SAA. 500 Revolver to
"A" Echelon 3rd Cav Brigade –
Amm[unitio]n Column send back 12 boxes
of 850 SAA
Capt Howard goes on leave & Lieut
Nisbet returns –
The lorry that went to St Omer for
Coal broke a front Spring (flaw) –

8th June Tuesday.
Fort Rouge.
Orderly officer Lieut Rubury.
Draw 4000 Francs from Field Cashier.
8 men go on leave at 8.P.M.
Send to Steenbecque for mortar bombs
to hand over to Railhead. & keep on Park
2 boxes Very flares 1 red 1 green & 4 Boxes
of red & green Rockets.
Thunder storm in the afternoon.
Lorry draws 25000 rounds SAA from
Strazeele.

9th June Wednesday.
                    Fort Rouge
Orderly Officer Lieut Nisbet —
Send off hind wheel rations lorry to
Steagall to be retyred —
Send schedule of Bills for a&d stores
to D.O.O. 2nd Ca Div for counter signature
Wheel returned retyred —
6 am Pte Downs brought for court martial
tomorrow morning at 11. a.m.
Men returned off furlough —
Drill & bathing Parade at 8 am
& 4 P M —

10th June   Thursday.
                    Fort Rouge
Orderly officer 2nd S.M. Hardy.
Send in Diary for May.
& Claims for May.
Court Martial of Pte Downsborough
at 4th Hussars at 11. am return at
4.30 PM.
Small Vauxhall M. 1786 - breaks
down - ball race gone in gear
box.
Parade ordered for Inspection of Kit
on Saturday 12th June

11th June Friday.
Fort Rouge
Orderly officer Lieut Rubury.
Send in returns & schedule for
supplies.
One lorry to be at Ebblinghem 8.30 am
for D.O.O. & to did.
Four old tyres sent to ado. Base.
Send in Parade state for tomorrows
inspection.
Lieut Rubury goes on leave.
Capt Howard returns from leave.
Draw 4000 francs from field Cashier

12th June Saturday.
Fort Rouge
Orderly officer Lieut Nisbet.
Send in stable returns.
Parade & inspection by O-in-C at
12 mid day. Leave at 10.30 am &
return at 2 P.M.
Send in Imprest acc. balance due
to Paymaster. 388 francs.
Inspect petrol. only 3rd Grade but
no complaints as such.
Oil poor

13th June Sunday

Orderly officer 2nd Lm. Hardy. Fort Rouge

Return of motor cycles sent to the ask
Billeting return sent in also Aunty
Return 116. 13 pr only in Park.
With a little alteration can carry 8
tins of petrol on lorries as well as
1 oil & 2 water as suggested.

14th June Monday.
Fort Rouge.

Capt Howard Orderly Officer.

See & ask re cooperation for drill purposes.

Ask that a Coy & M.S need not be sent to Park as Act Sergt Vasey is being trained

Find out a mistake made in return A & B 213 on 8th May. & carried forward each week write to O/c Records pointing this out & submitting new return.

15th June Tuesday.
Fort Rouge —
Orderly officer Lt Nisbet.

Take in car return to A.D.O.J.S.& T. see
Gen Tajart re promotion.

Lieut Rubray returns from leave &
Lieut Mallows goes on leave —

Send a car to O.C. A.S.C. from 2P.M.
to 8.P.M.

Some hand grenades handed over to
Railhead Thiézule by Pack in dangerous
condition. Report these were handed over
by D.O.O. at Steenbecque & taken
straight to Thiézule —

Draw 10 boxes of mortar amm" from
Thiézule.

16th June Wednesday
Fort Rouge —
Orderly officer M.S.M. Hardy —
In Park 99 rifles — 66 bayonets

Issue 10 000 S.A.A. to 20th Hussars
explosive draw & issued to 3rd Hussars —
Issue 7000 S.A.A. 16 bones 13p. to
Auxt Column —
Draw 2250 sd bags — 27 bxes flares
540 grenades No. 3 & distribute to units —
Orders received to stand by in readiness
to move in 2½ hrs notice —
Send 10 lorries to 20th Hussars to take
men to canal to bathe —
Draw 2000 francs from Field Cashier

17th June Thursday —
Fort Rouge —
Orderly officer Capt Howard —
Receive Halley Nos. 6816 & 2160.
from G.H.Q. for extra S.aa. drew
132 000 S.aa. to complete also drew
500 rounds 13 pr. HE from th[e] Zulu-
land 4 lorries to 20th Hussars —

18th June Friday -
Fort Rouge -
Orderly Officer Lt Rubury.
Send in schedule of Supplies.
Major Hitchman arrives about 10. am
gives orders re painting lamps & petrol
tins etc.
Issue 360 rounds 13pr H.E. to Column
& bring back 360 rounds shrapnel.
Vauxhall M1696. has a cracked Valve
seating 3rd Cylinder exhaust.
Send lorry No. 6816 to be relined at
Hazebrouck — A few minor things
require to be done to that lorry.

19th June Saturday.
Fort Rouge.

Orderly Officer Lt. Nisbet.

Draw 2000 francs from Field Cashier.

Draw 57000 rounds S.A.A. & 1776 revolver amm̄. issued to Amm̄ Column & units —

Draw 12 boxes bombs 95mm & issue to 3rd Cav Brigade —

Receive a wire at 6.P.M from Ettaquele ordering me to return the bomb amm̄. Take the matter to a.a. & d.M.G. who took the matter up —

Send in returns etc.

20th June Sunday Fort Raye

Orderly officer Lieut Rubury.
Lieut Meallows R.S.A. returned off leave
last night. Capt Goldsmith goes on leave

Daimler sent to C.R.A. for the day.
Paid out men going on leave.
Sent in Ans & Billeting returns to
A.A. & Q.M.G.

21st June Monday.
Orderly officer Lieut Nesbit — Fort Rouge
Daimler Car goes into workshops.
Drill & bathing parade as usual.
Lieut Nesbit goes into St Omer to buy some nails, for petrol carriers being made for all the lorries in the workshops.

22nd June Tuesday.
Orderly officer Lieut Nisbet vice Lt Rutley- Fort Rouge.

Car b.o.r. o.t.c at 9.30 am & returned at 12.30 P.m —

One lorry to St Omer & then to Hazebrouck for ordnance Stores etc.

L/Cpl Edwards deprived of lance stripe & given 14 days No.1 Field Pun. for insubordination to an N.C.O

23rd June Wednesday.
                    Fort Rouge.
Orderly officer Lieut Railway vice Le Mesurier
Lorry to Bethune for Hand grenades
for R.E.
Report to a.d. of S&T. on petrol reserve
Each lorry carries 16 galls in tank
16 gallons in tins. & 300 gall in head
quarters.
Rifles ordered to be handed in one per
lorry & car.
Drill & bathing parade as usual.

20th June Thursday.
Orderly officer Lieut Mobet.   Fort Rouge.
From Field Cashier — 500 francs.
" ———————— 5000 francs.

Four lorries to 20th Hussars for bathing
party. Pay men going on leave.
Lorry to Omer with men going on leave.

25th June Friday.
                              Fort Rouge.
Orderly officer Lieut Rubury.
One lorry to Strazeele to draw bombs
for 4th & 5th Brigades.
Issue 24000 S.A.A. to 12th Lancers.
— — 90000 S.A.A & 3000 Webley to
Anti Column. Lorries refil.

20th Hussars come for 19000 rounds
S.A.A. Schedule for supplies sent
in.
Pay out the Company.

26th June Saturday.
                                    Fort Rouge.
Orderly officer Lieut Nesbit.
13 pr. H.E increased to 15% of total carried
in Division draw 992 rounds & issue
108 rounds to each battery & 396 to Column
& keep 272 on park.
Draw 19000 rounds S.A.A. Withdraw from
batteries & equal amount of Shrapnel in
place of H.E.
On Park 1180 rounds Shrapnel.
            412   "   H.E.
Daimler car out of workshop & sent to
C.R.A. 2nd Div.
Returns etc sent in.

27

24th June Sunday.
      Fort Rouge.

Orderly Officer Lieut. Rubury.

Capt. Goldsmith returns from leave.

Capt. Howard proceeds on leave.

352 rounds 13 pr. Shrapnel drawn from Railhead. by order.

Ammunition return & billeting return sent in.

Bayonets sent in to complete the rifles sent in on 26th/7

28th June Monday.
Fort Rouge.

Orderly officer xxxx his bit.

Back axle for petrol lorry arrived — with spare wheels. Wheels & the old axle to be used for the water cart.

Pte Innes drunk & given 14 days No 1 Field punishment.

Pay men going on leave.

Lorries to be painted with numbers on the tail board. Motor cycles to be painted. Each Park & Colm to number from 1 to ——.

29th June Tuesday.
Fort Rouge.

Orderly officer M.J.M Hardy.

Issue 8000 SAA & 476 Revolver to 20th Hussars
& 15000 SAA to 6th Lancers.

Men return from leave. Pte Harley given
leave by War office till 30th June.

Pte Piper absent.

100 rounds for cattle killer asked
for. Not at Railhead at Supply.

Change back axle on petrol lorry.

Petrol racks being put on lorries.

30th June. Tuesday. Wednesday.
                    Fort Rouge.

Orderly Officer Lieut Rusbury.

Draw Detonators & Sand bags & issue to units
according to list.

Returns for the end of the month sent
in.

Authority received to forward billeting
returns prior to March 1st.

Send Interpreter round to make
enquiries as regards names etc.

           C.L. Goldsmith Capt
                    A.S.C.
           O.C. 2nd Cdn Div Amn Park.

2-7-15.

121/6401

2nd Cavalry Division

2nd Cav Div Ammn Park

G O C

1-3-07-15

31

1st July Thursday.
Fort Rouge.

Orderly officer Lieut Nisbet –
Draw 2000 Francs from Field Cashier
Send a lorry to Vieux Berquin to collect
rifles etc left in that district by troops –
Have to send a car for the use of
No 2 Field Squadron for 3 weeks. Through
R. A. S. C.
Piper absent from leave. Forfeits 2 days pay
+ 14 days No 1 Field Punishment –
Receive 2 boxes gun cotton primers
from Doo for 16th Lancers.

2º July Friday
                    Fort Rouge.
Orderly officer M.S.M Hardy.
Send in diary for June —
Pay out men going on leave —
Send old rifles etc to Railhead —
Send in trading Strength + Schedule of
supplies —
Capt Howard returns from leave but
Rubury proceeds on leave —

3rd July Saturday Fort Rouge.

Orderly officer Capt Howard.

Issue 20.000 SAA & 2 boxes revolver Amt. to Amt Column.

Draw 19000 SAA & one full box was collected at Kun Buquin on 1st

Capt Goldsmith goes round all old billets to find out names of house holders.

Issue 2 boxes pinion to 16th Hussars & 5 lbs black powder to 4th Huss. & 16th Lancers.

Returns as usual. 5 men join from M.T. Base.

4th July   Sunday.
                Fort Rouge.
Orderly officer Lieut Nisbet.
Parade at 8 am for inspection of the
old & new rifles etc. All new short rifles
to be handed in.
Church parade in orders for 6 P.M at
Ant Park billets. Parson did not turn up.
Ant return & billeting return sent in

5th July Sunday. Fort Rouge -
Orderly officer M S M Hardy.
Capt Goldsmith member of Court martial
at Anti Column at 10 am.

Another 10% of H.E. to be drawn reserve
103 rounds per battery. 394 to Column
4 lorries leave at 8.am & take 208
rounds 13pr Shrapnel to railhead as that
amount will be surplus when the 13pr
S is returns in place of H.E. Park now
full _ 202 F.S. 672 H.E.
Water Cart completed with lorry back
axle & wheels.

6th July Tuesday.
                    Fort Rouge
Orderly officer Capt Howard –
Capt. Goldsmith goes to Wizerne to find
names of billets etc –

D of T. Inspects Park at 1 P.M. Capt.
Goldsmith not present. remarks Petrol
tins with oil & water to have the handles
reversed. his opinion is they won't stand
the weight –

83 rifles short. & 47 bayonets
sent to O.O Havre in 3 cases.
receipt taken from R.T.O.

7th July Wednesday
Orderly Officer Lt Violet — Fort Rouge
Amt. Return sent in 5.00 in charge
at 12 noon. full up.
Ast. Col. asked for 85 000 Saa at
12-45 P.M. Me Long drew 85000 from
Railhead.
Drew 6000 francs from Pay master
Lieut Rubury returned from leave
Billeting return from 1st billet to
9th march sent in, each commune
on separate page. Copies kept.

8th July Thursday
                    Fort Rouge.
Orderly officer M.S.M. Hardy.
Lieut Nisbet goes on leave to catch
1.5. am boat tomorrow morning.
Send wine bills to D.O.O. for countersignature
The wheels ^back axle etc of water cart
handed over to O.O. Steenbeeque.
Pay out the company.

9th July Friday.   Fort Rouge.
Orderly officer Captain Howard
Q.L 4196/4. Another 10 % HE to be drawn
972 rounds Shrapnel returned to Railhead —
+HE drawn in its place. 104 to each battery
393 to Amn. Colm + 267 for Park.
In Park. 1760 Sh: & 940. HE —
Return motor cycles   to OC a/c
—— feeding strength   o/c Supplies
Schedule of Supplies —

10th (Saturday) July.

Orderly officer Lieut Rubury. Fort Rouge

Stables went in.

Take stabs to A Sqn S&T.

Drills as usual.

~~Rec~~ Punishment given by Capt
Howard to L/Cpl Edwards viz.
Deprived of Lance Stripe & 14 days No.1 FP
illegal - write to obtain G.O.C's authority
to cancell the 14 days.

11th July Sunday.
                    Fort Rouge.
Orderly Officer M.S.M Hardy.
Billeting return & Amn. Return sent in.
Collect Some private property of Lieut
G. P Armstrong 34th Shiko. killed on
2nd July.
Coy Sgt Major has a bad wrist from fall
rather serious.
No Church Parade.

12th July. Monday.

Orderly Officer Capt Howard – Fort Rouge.
Drills as usual.
Pay out two men going on leave.
Send in Imprest Acc. Balance due to
Paymaster 1752 - 55.

13th July Tuesday
Fort Rouge

Orderly Officer Lieut Rubney.
hon: Paulmier goes on leave.
Capt Howard sick with toothache —
Send up petrol lorry at 9.30 P.M. to
refil lorries with 2d Field Squadron
Award of L/Cpl Edwards to be cancelled
by order of Maj General Kavanagh
Comd 2d Cav Div —

14th July Wednesday
                    Fort Rouge.

Orderly Officer 2/Lt M. Hardy.
Forwarded to Regt Pay master a War Loan
demand for Pte L. G. Hopkins No MM/07370
for £20. AB64 written up.
Lieut Nisbet returns from leave.

15th July Thursday
Fort Rouge

Orderly officer Capt Howard.
Drills as usual.
Car sent to A.D.O.S. 2nd Div.
A.D.M.S. inspected Park requires more
latrines to be made —
Nisbet goes to St Anne to purchase split
peas etc. A case from Commercial
Motor received —

16th July Friday
                Fort Rouge
Orderly officer Lieut Rubury.
5000 rounds SAA to Anti Column
Lieut Mallows + one man pass on
leave.
Fuding strength + motor bicycle return
Sent in.
Drills as usual.

17th July Saturday — Fort Rouge.

Orderly officer Lieut Nisbet

Too wet for drill.

Returns sent in.

One lorry comes in from 2nd Field Squadron to be relieved. Capt Howard goes to inspect the roads. Reports that the roads are unfit for lorries are in a very bad condition.

Send the lorry to be relieved.

Send staff by Lt Rubury to Dorfgut.

Men complain about their rations with 2nd Field Squadron.

18th (Sunday) July.

Fort Rouge

Orderly officer Lt S.M. Hardy.
Receive orders to complete to 50% of HE
Send five lorries with 1492 Shrapnel under
Lt Rubruy at 8.a.m. As Amn Return
is due. showed the HE as having been
drawn at 12 mid day. Owing to fire
at RE Park Strozulle lorries did not
return till 10. P.M. 28 rounds HE under
drawn. Issued & recharged with units
600 Amn Col. 159"D" 162"E" 159"J"
Billeting return sent in —

19th July. Monday.

Orderly officer Capt Howard. Fort Rouge.

The Am'n Railhead issued 28 rounds short yesterday of H.E.

O.O Strozule will come when it is available.

See Q and M.G. about Lorries with 2: Field Squadron, + ask if constructional Lorries can not be obtained + these lorries of mine are spare + should not be used for this purpose —

20th July Tuesday
                    Fort Rouge.
Orderly officer Lieut Rubury.
hon: Paulanier returnes from leave.
A.D. of S & T visits Park, requires a
detail kept of petrol consumption.
Receive note from A.A.& Q.M.G. that no
construction lorries are available so that
mine will not be relieved with 2nd Fus
Squadron
Drills as usual.

21st July Wednesday

Fort Rouge

Orderly officer Lieut Nisbet —
M.S.M. Hardy goes on leave —
C.O. Stagpole wires 2F rounds HE
available at Ant. Railhead —
Jo to see O.C. ASC 2nd Cav Div in morning
& to 2nd Field Squadron in the afternoon
Lorries likely to be used another two
weeks at least. Roads not so bad as
they have moved to Kemmel district.
exchanged car drivers —

22ᵈ July Tuesday.   52

Orderly officer Capt Howard. Fort Rouge.
Make out manuscript Book for petrol per
mile per week for lorries —
Drew 6000 Francs from Paymaster &
paid out the Company —

23rd July Friday.
Fort Rouge.
Orderly Officer Lieut Rubury.
Purchase wood for cook stove lorry.
Send lorry to St Omer to draw the wood
Send in schedule & feeding strength
10 men arrive from Base.
Only five men Cat "C" willing to take
on for duration of the war.
Capt Colquhoun talks to Cat "C" men
and men are to sign on on the 27th.

24th July Saturday

Fort Rouge

Orderly officer Lieut Mislet.

Send nominal Roll of gunners to Paymaster. Dover.

Ammⁿ Park to carry 243,000 rounds S.a.a short as Reg^t are carrying 27000 rounds each surplus. Send out lorries to adjust — Total returned to Railhead 305,260 rounds S.a.a.

Returns made out & sent to ad of sd.

Drills as usual during week.

10 men join th^e Park from Base on 23rd

25th July Sunday. Fort Rouge
Orderly Officer Captain Howard.
Church Parade 10.30 am under O.Officer
for C.ofE & 6 P.M. Presbyterians.
Billeting return made out & countersign'd
by Mayor. AB. 397 used.
Am[mun]t[ion] return sent in.
Report to AA & QMG. completion of the
exchange & new adjustment of S.A.A.
2nd Corps Troop. S.C. give us a single
Halley Cylinder.

26th July Monday
                              Fort Rouge.
Orderly officer Lieut Rubury.
Copy of billeting return sent to AA & QMG
Capt. Goldsmith inspects lorries at
Kemmel on detachment — Instruct Cpl
I/C to keep petrol & mile account.
DOO gives verbal permission for Pack
to purchase wood for store lorry. Bill
to be countersigned by DOO
Wood purchased in St Omer.

27th July Tuesday   57

Orderly Officer Lieut Mabet. Fort Rouge.

14 Category 'C' men sign AFW 3125
wire sent to O/C A&C Records accordingly.
Instruction to wire nos on the 26th only received
this morning —

Command Paymaster Base returns form for
War Loan of Pte Hopkins. Return to be
made out on AFW 3143 & 3144 wire to
Stationery Depot for forms as none have
been issued & Paymaster has none.

28th July Wednesday   58

Orderly officer M.S.M Hardy —   Fort Rouge

Five more men category 'C' sign at W
3125 — Capt. Goldsmith hands over 1010 Frs
to Capt. Howard answering for him on leave.
Pte Ellison reported for fast driving
Car No 1910 with C.R.A.

The 10 men who joined on 26th had short
rifles. These are sent to the AOD ~~Have~~
Base — receipt obtained from R.T.O

29th July Thursday.   **59**

Orderly officer Lieut Rubury — Fort Rouge

Capt Howard to Lorries on detachment
Cpl Mohrmann & Pte Wheeling sign on
for duration of war —
Pte Ellison 8 days No 2 Field Punt
for driving a car at excessive speed
reported by D A D O f S of T — EC.
Pte Ellison on detachment with CRA

30th July Friday.   60

Orderly officer Lieut Nisbet.   Fort Rouge

Men on detachment paid out —
Petrol lorry sent up to Kemmel with
petrol for lorries on detachment —
Schedule for Supplies sent in —
also feeding strength —
Drills as usual + bathing Parade —

31st July Saturday.
Fort Rouge

Orderly Officer M.S.M Hardy.

Pte Stewart Category "C" sent to England for discharge - with written instr. to report to O.C 52 M.T. Coy ASC Aldershot.

Lieut Mallows to Lieut Col to exchange 4 rounds H.E. defective - took 5500 rounds S.A.A to Steezeele (loose) -

Returns sent in for week

A.R. Goldsmith Capt.
ASC.
OC 2nd Cav Div Ammunition Park

121/8695

2nd Cav: Division

2nd Cav: Div: Amm" Park.

Vol X

1 - 31. 8. 15.

2ⁿᵈ August Monday.
Fort Rouge.

Orderly officer Lieut Nisbet.
One lorry sent to R E to take material
for roofing to do Clyte & Deanoutre.
1 lorry to draw 9 boxes hand grenades
from Strazeele for 2ⁿᵈ Field Squadron
under Lieut Mallows.
Billeting return signed & forwarded to
A.A. & Q.M.G.

3ʳᵈ August Tuesday
                                    Fort Rouge
Orderly officer M.S.M. Hardy.

AB 213 A returned from A&Q of SoT last
how Rank & file 103 was arrived at.

4 Cars   4 —
27 lorries   54 —   50 % taken of
Batmen   4   total strength of Rank
Cpl   4   103   & file vide provisional
Spare 50%   33   War Est. sent round.
2 Cltr lorries 4

Supply Railhead changed to Arques.

Lt Nisbet goes to La Clytte. with openings
for lorries on detachment.

4th August Wednesday

Orderly Officer Capt Howard. Fort Royé

Capt Goldsmith returned from leave at mid-night
Parades as usual.
4 lorries asked for to move Div. 2 for RE
1 for E Battery & 1 for Head Quarters & A&MG.
at different hours - on 5th
Daily returns of lorries & cars to be kept
by section officers -

5th August Thursday
                    Fort Rouge
Orderly officer Lieut Rubury.

Pte Piper up for absence from 6.30am till 12.30pm
Forfeits 1 days pay + 4 days No-1 F.P. sent
to A.P.M.

Capt Howard goes on leave.

Div. will not move till 6th towards area.

6th August, Friday.
                    Fat Rouge.
Orderly officer Lieut Nisbet.
Send in Schedule for supplies &
feeding strength.
Busy making out petrol consumption

7th August. Saturday.
Fort Rouge.
Orderly Officer M.S.M Hardy.
Make out AB 213.a — & send in the
copies. Make up petrol book. Miles
per gall for the Park very bad. Send
Lt. Nisbet out on 5743 on petrol test &
result 7 miles per 2 gall. While 6088
shows 7 miles per gall.
Draw 400 kilos coal and make
arrangements with R.A.M.C. to disinfect
the clothes etc of the Park. To start
at 7 am tomorrow 30 men at a time.

8th August Sunday
Fat Rouge.

Orderly officer Lieut Rubery.
Make out Billeting returns get it signed by mayor & send duplicate to aa & QMG.
Go to see ADof S&T re log books. See if daily or weekly miles can be put down.
Draw 2150 Francs require 6000 Paymaster has no more to draw at 9.30. 10th Draw 3360 Very flares from S.to gule
Another front spring on lorries at La Clytte broken send Lt Nisbet up with new one. Receive plan of new billeting area.
See AD of S&T re men Category "C" going on leave.

9th August Monday

Orderly officer Lieut Nisbet. Fort Rouge.

All men not disinfected yesterday went up at 9.30 am. All lorries washed out with Creosol. Manure heaps etc also sprayed with creosol solution.

Spare men for Company are to be reduced at 50% of drivers of Motor lorries only. Number for Park. 29 not 33 vide WO letter I have never seen.

Halley 6087 comes in from Field Squadron to be retyred.

10th August Tuesday_

Orderly officer ~~to~~ M.S.M. Hardy_ Fort Rouge_
Draw 4000 francs from Paymaster.
See adopt & t. Get permission to keep
mileage by week instead of daily_
Summary of mileage to be shown_
Halley 6087 sent to be retyred at
Thiazule both hind wheels. Also broken
spring replaced. ~~P~~
Pay out the Company at 5. P.M_
make the following promotions_

L.Cpl Louick to Cpl.   8.F.15.
" "   Moure   "
" "   Burton   "
Pte   Richardson L.Cpl.
"   Irwin   "
"   Asgathorp   "

72

11th August Wednesday.

Fort Rouge.

Orderly officer Lieut Rusbury.

Halley 6087 G returns to La Clytte with petrol, oil & paraffin –

Send in diary to G Base –

Lieut Mallows takes 360 Flares to 5th Lancers & 16th Hussars & Capt'd 240 –

Capt Howard returns from leave

Send bills to D.O.O. for countersignature.

Lieut Mallows goes to arrange exchange of HE at present with units with HE which has been examined – On return wire arrives to say 600 rounds 13 pr. HE now available for exchange.

12th August Thursday 73
Fort Rouge

Orderly officer Lieut Nisbet –
Lieut Mallon's takes 2 lorries HE to
Thiozule for exchange. 600 rounds &
then to CRA to distribute as required.
Also 360 Flares to units each 4th Brigade
E battery completed.

Pte Warren G & Pte Warren H both
up for absence. 7 days No2 F.P. &
sent to A.P.M

13th August Friday.
                    Fort Rouge.
Orderly Officer R.S.M Hardy.
J. Battery 13pr HE exchanged.
Fighting strength & Schedule of supplies
forwarded to D.T S.O.

Lieut Rubury starts on leave.

75

14th August Saturday.

Fort Rouge.

Orderly officer Capt Howard.
Send Imprest Acc away balance due
to Paymaster 899 Francs 45 —
Enquiries &c sent to D Battery.
& 212 horses to Amn Column.
Full loads drawn. Amn Column
require 166 horses to complete.
Send in state &c. Total strength
of Park to be 122 all told & 99 Rank & File
Percentage of spare men to be 50% of lorry
drivers only. —

15th August Sunday.
Orderly officer Lt: Nisbet. Fort Rouge _

Send to mayor billeting return & get duplicate
signed _ Report on Am̅t̅ return all
H̅t̅ now being examined _
Make out mileage return _ 5·94 miles per
gall used for 24 lorries _ 13 galls used by
8 lorries which did not move _
Draw explosives as laid down for the
Park to carry _
Despatch old stores etc to M.T. Base
AB 108. 1 + 2.

77

16th August. Monday
                                    Fnt Rouge.
Orderly officer M.S. M Hardy.
Report Park complete in exploders HE
to CRA & complete in explosives to
AA & 8 M.G. + T.O.O.
Send in duplicate bulletin, return to Div.
M2/2692 Pte Lawson absent. Forfeits 2 days Pay
+ 7 days No.1 F.P. Pte Lunn absent Forfeits
1 days Pay + 7 days No.1 F.P. both sent
to A.P.M.

17th August Tuesday
Fort Rouge
Orderly Officer Capt Howard.
Draw 750 Sandbags & certain explosives
reissued as detailed.
Gunners Logan & Wright absent 8 days No
2 F.P. & forfeit 1 days Pay R.W.
9465 — Cpl Buntin on leave to England
for 1 month due back 17 9/15.

18th August Wednesday.
                    Fort Rouge -

Orderly officer Lieut Nisbet -

Arrange new system of keeping equipment acc.
NCO/c Store to enter daily. Articles used or
material expended & Corry expended on -
O/c Workshop to strike off weekly in ledger.

C/978 L/Cpl Asgathorp)
C/741 Pte Lark   ) to England on 1 month
C/745 " Forrest   ) leave due back
C/761 " Northam   ) 18/9/15.

Capt Howard draws 2000 francs for
Park -

19th August Thursday.
Fort Rouge
Orderly officer M.S.M. Hardy.
Send in indents for M.T. Stores cancelling
all previous demands.

D.a.a.+Q.M.G. Cav. Corps came round re
H.E. & S. Pack now to carry 87 rounds per
gun H.E. & 63. S. moves & alterations
in H.E. & S to be ordered by Corps only.
Other orders to come from Division.

Lieut Rubury returns from leave.

Send Petrol, oil etc up to Lorries with
Field Squadron.

20th August Friday
Fort Rouge

Orderly Officer Capt Howard.

C/1986. Pt Whirling start on 1 months leave
21-8-15 to 20-9-15.

Old boots which are unpassable to be sent to
Qtr Column. Explosives etc to complete units
available to Schedule.

Send in schedule of supplies to the
Troops Supply Officer also estimated requirements
of wood & coal. Wood 3000 this dispu month
coal

31st August Saturday
Fort Rouge

Orderly officer Lieut Rubury.

Send one lorry with 524 boxes Shrapnel
to exchange for 524 boxes H.E. at 8.a.m
make out returns etc.

Lieut Nisbet draws 6000 francs for O.C
Park.

Lieut Nisbet goes on leave.

Pay out the company.

Lieut Mallows draws explosives etc to
complete unit to G.1098.

Three lorries leave for 2nd Field Squadron
making total 6 lorries on construction
8 R.E. from Park.

22nd August. Sunday

Orderly Officer M.S.M Hardy. Fort Rouge

Send Ammⁿ return etc in.

Lieut Mallows goes round units with explosives etc –

Wire comes in to report No of shells HE with 44-80 on the case – Lt Mallows does not return till 5 P.M. only half the shells examined before dark.

Sgt Randall comes in to report. Front spring housing broken & springs going on 6 Ton lorry. also flexible tubing for Clutch drip feed broken. He takes out new parts.

Billeting return signed by Mayor.

Order to change 72 rounds per battery HE into Shrapnel.

23rd August Monday

Fort Rouge.

Orderly officer Capt Howard.

Examination of shells continued. Wire number to A.a.&Q. M.G. 8 a.m. send lorry round to exchange 72 rounds HE to S with each battery. 150 Smoke helmets received.

Send 1 spare lorry to replace 6 Tonner with 2nd Field Squadron.

2 P.M. Send Lt Rubury to inspect lorries at 2nd Field Squadron.

Motor Cycle No. 7 damaged.

Give damaged Halley B Type gear-box to 3rd Corps Troops Supply Column.

24th August Tuesday

Fort Rouge
Orderly officer Lieut Rubury

Report to OC RHA 2 Ca Div. complaint
with No. 241/3. d/ 22.8.15.

Authority for demanding AB 395. to
AD to Stationery Services No 83/1. dated 19-8-15.

~~[struck out]~~

Correspondence re pay of Tuohy & Pearson returns
copy of advertisement to be forwarded.

Drew 5000 francs from Field Cashier —

86

25th August Wednesday.

Fort Rouge

Orderly officer M.S.M Hardy.

Capt Howard inspects lorries with 2. F.S.

Sends in Lorry No.   with damaged spring & steering defective

Respiration tube retained until 2. Smoke helmet is issued.

Supply column 2 Cav Div. receive radiator lamps etc for Halleys struck off in day issue book.

87

26th August Thursday.
Fort Rouge

Orderly Officer Capt Howard
Lieut Risley takes out No 2 Section —
Demonstration to be held on 2nd Sept will
now be held at Oxford Hussars & not at
Hd Qrs 4" C.B. as directed —
Stores arrive from M.T. Depot.
Batteries ordered to move — No orders yet
for Park

27th August. Friday.
Fort Rouge

Orderly Officer Lieut. Rubury.

Pte MY/049523 W. Wood arrived from Base.

Send in schedule of supplies —

Draw 600 kilos. wood from Wood in Clairmarais.

No civilian labour used —

Capt. Goldsmith goes to Vieux Berquin to obtain duplicate of Bill lost —

Capt. Howard takes out No. 1 Section lorries —

88

28th August Saturday
                    Fort Rouge
Orderly Officer M.S.M. Hardy.
Lieut Nisbet returns from leave.
Make out states etc.
Make up petrol consumption. Lorries
5-46 miles per gall.

29th August Sunday.
                    Fort Rouge.
Orderly Officer Capt Howard —
Capt Goldsmith to see AA+QMG at
9.a m. Batteries move on 4th
Anti Park 13 pr lorries to 2nd Anti
Sub Park St Venant.

30th August Monday.
                    Fort Rouge
Orderly officer Lieut Rubury.
Order received for Park to exchange all
13pr HE with batteries & Column not marked
44/80. Send Lorries to Steenwerck only
400 rounds available —
Number to be exchanged — Batteries 804
Column 1580. Park 1346 — Total 3730 —

31st August Tuesday.
                    Fort Rouge.
Orderly Officer Lieut. Nisbet.
No 13pr HE 44/80 available at Shozul
Pay out the Park.
Draw fuze etc from Railhead
for D.O.O.
Issue 100 rifle grenades to units
as detailed by D.O.O.
Routine Order No. 041. 3 Copies a/fB213
to be sent to AA & Q. M. G. 2 Cav Div.
Q.L. 5037. d/30.8.15 Says it will not be
necessary for me to send one now direct
to O/c A.S.C. Records A.G.'s office –
140 Rounds Revolver Amt. Issued to
Camp Commandant.

                    C.E. Goldsmith Capt
                            ASC
                    O.C. 2 Cav Div Amt Park

1-9-15.

1st August Sunday.

Fort Rouge

Orderly Officer Lieut Rubney.

Start drawing rations on AB.55.

Billeting return sent in. Mayor was out so could not be signed.

Amt return sent in.

L. Mallows to Battn. + Amn Column re exchange of HE for inspection.

C of E Parade under orderly Officer at 10.30 a.m.

Non conformist parade at 6.0 P.M. under orderly Sergt.

121/6973

2nd Cavalry Division

2nd Chev: Div: Anm: Park

Vol XII

Sept. 15

Diary for September 1915

1st September — ~~Tuesday~~ Wednesday — Fort Rouge

Orderly officer ~~Lieut Nisbet~~ — M.S.M. Hardy —
Orders received that 13 pr HE fuses need not be exchanged
Lorry 3041 — on detachment breaks a spring & the
driver looses control & dashes into a wall —
Lieut Nisbet goes up to bring lorry in. Damage to
lorry front axle bent both springs broken —
Daimler Car M.1910 showing very bad petrol
consumption this car detached with R. RHA
2nd Cav Div —
Vauxhall Car in shops with weak springs
— No. 1786 — Smiths break one trying to jump
them —
Purchase spring steel (8 francs) for Vauxhall

2ⁿᵈ September – ~~Wednesday~~ Thursday   Fort Rouge.

Orderly Officer ~~M.S. — Hardy~~ – Capt Howard
Parade at 10 a.m. for Demonstration in the
use of Smoke Helmets 4 Officers 90 O.R.
attend Party returns at 2. P.M.
D.O.O. draws 96 slabs of dry wet. gun cotton to
issue to units.

No orders received about the move of the Park
So indent for rations for 4ᵗʰ

Lieut Nisbet carries out test for petrol consumption for Daimler No 17 19·10 miles per
gall on 2 gall test was 22 miles per gall

No drill parade today.

3rd September. Friday —   Fort Rouge.

Orderly Officer ~~Capt~~ Lieut Rubrey —
Capt Howard goes to see damage done by
lorry 30421 — As the lorry was working under orders
of 2nd Field Squadron they will arrange claim —
Send in Claim for officers allowances —
Still no orders for move so indent for 5th
Orders received to examine all H.E. 13 pr
to see if they can be set between 0 & 2.
Those that can are to be exchanged —
No keys on the Park send to J. Battery RHA
for some — Too late to examine tonight —
At 6. P.M — Wire received from AA & QMG
asking what arrangement I have made & what
hour I move on 4th re our conversation. Reply
lorries will move at 1. P.M — but no orders
have been received as no date for move
of Park was known at time of conversation —
Issue instructions to Capt Howard who
is in charge of sect. Send Cycle orderly to
2nd Aux! Sub Park to ask if he can draw
rations for my section for 6th reply received
that he can —
M.S.M Hardy goes on leave —

4th September. Saturday Fort Rouge –

Orderly officer Lieut Nisbet –
Draw & issue 5000 SAA + 500 Revolver to
Oxford Hussars.
Draw corrugated iron from R.E Park Steenwerck
issue to wood cutting Party at Claremarais –
Send Diary for August to DAG Base –
Send AFB 213 A direct to O/c ASC Section to
prevent mistake. 3 copies to AA+QMG &
one copy to ADofS of T. One office copy –
Work out petrol consumption for week –
Lorries – 5·37 M pg.s } 16 galls running engines
Cars – 16·10   —   } 359½ gall. 1931 miles
Following go on detachment – 2 officers (1 ASC.
1 RFA) 3 Sergts (1 RFA) 22 Drivers 14 RFA.
2 Car Drivers – 2 artificers 2 Cooks 1 servant
4 Spare men (1 Cpl. 2 L Cpl 1 driver) –
11 Lorries 2 Cars 2 Motor Cycles –
Pte White goes to Amt Column –
Pte Bailey W G granted extension of leave till
8th Sept by Records on account of wife's illness.

One smoke helmet per man issued to men on
detachment.

5th September Sunday. Fort Rouge

Orderly officer Lieut Rubery.
Make out billeting return total payment — 66.36 Francs
Send to OO Calais — Tackles differential 2 Ton —
Drill post 2¼" — Tube expander — Chest tool — cutting
tubes 1¾" to 3" — Key sent under separate cover —
Letter received from Editor Sunday Chronical that no
advertisement for ASC wheelers was issued before the
end of March at 5/- per day in his paper —
Send Nisbet to detachment with Car 1786 to bring
back Car 1696 — List of stores taken out of store
see end of book.
A.F.B 122 for men on detachment sent to Capt Howard
Received orders to send a fatigue party to
Wardrecques Supply Depot to off coal.
1 NCO & 10 men at 9 a.m order cancelled
time altered to 2 P.M.
The five lorries at detachment with 2d
Field Squadron return at 4.30 P.M —
Sgt Randall in charge

6th September Monday
Fort Rouge
Orderly Officer Lieut Nisbet.
Receive order to say how much "B" SAA
on charge. Send Rubrey to Eliazule to find
out exactly what "B" SAA was. It is
marked on list $\overline{VII}$ & a letter B. 'K'. G.E.
etc.
Send Paulimin with billeting return to get it
countersigned by the Mayor.
1 NCO & 10 men required for fatigue at 8.30
a.m.
B type SAA 58 boxes 1000 each one
box marked buried & one box 560 rounds.
Send lorry 2 P.M to collect 194. 75mm bombs
from Argues (000) take them to Eliazule & draw
200 new ones & distribute as detailed.
54 pairs of boots sent to OO Calais repair.

Lorry 6072 to Isberques for returning.
Detonators for time fuze for HE. 13 pr to be
removed

7th September Tuesday
Fort Rouge –

Orderly Officer Lieut Rubery –

Lieut Nisbet goes to Heavy Section. with log books completed up to date.

Reports on return that Daimler 1910 has not been returned by O.C. R.H.A

1 NCO & 15 men required at 8.30 am for fatigue.

Pay out detachment which returned from Kemmel –

Lorry distributing bombs returns having drawn 208 – Issued 147 & 61 remain on Park.

Report in re Capt Howard not having a pass when going to Kemmel on duty –

Receive schedule for supplies from O/c Supplies –

Univic car not returned from 2d Field Squadron –

Purchase spring steel & service paint in St Omer.

Send in report that I can not trace advertisement in daily papers prior to 20.3.15 in which wheelers are asked for at 5/- per day.

Lorry 6095 to Isbergues for retyring –
Time fuzes being taken out –

8th September Wednesday.
                                    Fort Rouge.
Orderly officer Lieut Nisbet.
Fatigue Party 1 NCO + 15 men at 8.30am.
Write to AA + Q MG for written authority for
Daimler Car to be detached while batteries are
in action. Also to O.C. ASC to ask when
Unic car will be returned.
Indent for 150 field Dressings.
No wood to be taken from Clairmarais forest
unless a receipt is given to NCO on duty there.
Address. C/o M Cousin, 1 Rue de Malhove Argues.
Issue 20000 SAA + 4 boxes revolver to
Amn Column.
A.F.G. 3156 return of motor Cars + A.F.W. 3157 return
of motor cycles to be rendered to reach ADof S't
's office by the 1st of each month.
Receive four copies of field Service pocket Book
Issue as follows 1 Capt Goldsmith 1 Lieut Rawling
1 L? Nisbet 1 office copy.

3 HE 13pr. Defective all other time fuzes taken
out.
160 rounds Shrapnel to Column
21 defective shells from Amn Column handed
over to Railhead St Venant.

Drew 24 Rounds HE 21pr Column + 3 Park
defective + 60 Shrapnel to inspect.

9th September Thursday
Fort Rouge.

Orderly Officer Lieut Rubury.
Capt Goldsmith to see AA & MG at 9 a.m. received instructions that no one had authority except AA & MG to order any of my cars or lorries out on any duty.
~~Daimler~~ Daimler Car to be returned by OC R H a ? Uric Car to be returned by OC 2d Field Squadron.
Go + inspect Heavy Section. Lorries very clean.
Draw 20,000 SAA + 6 boxes revolver Amm from Railhead.
Fatigue party 1 NCO + 15 men at 8.30 a.m.
A.D.M.S. inspects Park while I was away, certain things wrong.
Can not obtain any leather belting for fan belts by purchase.
Receive authority to purchase canvas for Latrine screens. from D.O.O.

10th September. Friday.
Fort Rouge.

Orderly Officer Lieut Nisbet.
Send lorry to Forest to draw wood –
Send in Schedule of Supplies to D.T.S.O
Send in 10 bills to be countersigned by D.O.O
Have to send to detachment for Pte Geddes to
be interviewed at Cav Corps Head Quarters re
engineering certificate.
No fatigue party today.

Purchase canvas for latrine screen at St.
Omer 30 francs – (2 bills).

11th September Saturday.
                                Fort-Rouge

Orderly officer Lieut Rodney.
Report from Capt Howard for the week arrives
all B type amn't Boxes to be marked in white
paint. M.G.B. Bills returned from too
few at 7.30 P.M. 100 detonators 120 Dry
primers & 16 fath. Fuze No-10. to be issued
to Royal Scots Greys. Send in a FB 213
1 to Div, 1 ADOSST & 1 To. Op ASC Sect'n Base
Div. Routine order on the subject to cancelled.
Make out petrol consumption.

Lorries - 234½ gall. 1257 miles = 5.33 M.P.G.
Cars   -   6 "   1112   " = 17.37 —

M.S.M. Hardy returns from leave —

Spreadh R. Regular Reserve T/   Roberts absent off
leave to England from   reported on a FB
213 4th AP.M —

12th September Sunday.
Fort Rouge.

Orderly officer Lieut Nisbet.
Made out billeting return. 57 francs 40.
Sent trans pos return to O.C. S.T.
Receive receipts from M.T. Base & O.C. Claim for stores forwarded.
Issue Detonators etc to Royal Scots Greys & 3 6mm revolver ant to 20th Hussars.
Exchange 25 6mm 'B' type ant Column with ant Column.
4 lorries at 2-45 P.M. at Argues to take machine guns round to units.
Fatigue party 1 NCO & 15 men to Waducqueres.
Four dial sights received for ant Column to be sent to heavy section.
Bills countersigned by D.O.O 190 Francs 30.
List at end of book.

13th September Monday.
Fort Rouge.

Orderly Officer M.S.M. Hardy.
Fatigue party 1 NCO + 15 men at 8.30 a.m.
Send Motor Cyclist to all units to find out the no.
of S.A.A. rounds "U" American to be exchanged —
  Issue 150 rounds S.A.A to H.Qrs 4th Cav Brigade
Report W.O.C. A.S.C. No 627 —
10 Cat "Z" due for discharge before 1st Jan. 6 extended 4
21 ———————————— after 1st " 16 — " —   5

Park has 9 boxes "U" Auti, S.A.A = 9000 rounds —
2 lorries to Parade at D.O.O Office Argues Fal-
3. O P.M — for stores etc —
14000 Rounds S.a.a Issued to Oxford Hussars

14th September Tuesday
                    Fort Rouge -
Orderly Officer Lieut ~~Hitchel~~ Rubray -
Park to carry 2 trench mortars for each Regt
+ 64 bombs 9.5 m— per regt —

Park to collect when ready —
Coal fatigue 1. N.C.O + 5 men at 8.30 a.m —

Send cyclist round all units to find out amount
of U amt but they don't know as yet —
Units can draw 20 rounds per rifle + 2000 per
gun 'B' Amt S.A. available at Steenjeele —

15th September Wednesday —
                              Fort Rouge
Orderly officer Lieut Nisbet.
Capt Goldsmith to see AA+QMG. 9. am
Draws 2000 Francs from Paymaster —
Lent in imprest acct. Balance due to
Paymaster on acc. 1415-55 Francs.
Exchange 360 rounds "U" SAA for 12th Lancers
2000. 6th DG — 720 3 Hussars — 1178
20th Hussars. 4000 Ant L Column.

Issue 24 boxes SAA to Ant Column &
4 boxes revolver — & 12 boxes 20th Hussars

Lieut Nisbet sick — slight attack of flue —
Coal fatigue 1 NCO + 15 men at 8.30 am.

16th September Thursday.
Fort Rouge

Orderly Officer M.S.M. Hardy.

See A & Q of 1st Cav Corps at 11 a.m. & then to a.a & Q M.G. 2nd Cav Div.

Arrange that when R.H.A car returns that the car is to stop with the Park & when O.C R.H.a requires one he can send for it.

Received from 3rd Hussars. 2 motors – 4 boxes of bomb amm̄ – 2 ramrods. 1 box gun cotton, 1 box detonators 8 boxes fuse.

Oxford Hussars. 2 motors. 6 boxes bomb am̄, 1 box 15 rounds. 6th D.G 2 motors 1 ramrod 6 boxes Am̄ +

Exchange 628 rounds "U" with 5th Lancers.

Send testimonial for wife of Sgt Randall to to O/c A.S.C. Section.

Send Sheets A.F.N 1573 Nos 9 to 13 d/ 4-3-15

to Paymaster I/c clearing House total payments 4225 francs.

Coal fatigue 1.NCO + 15 men at 8.30 a.m

17th September Friday
Fort Rouge.

Orderly Officer Lieut Rubury
Coal Fatigue 1 NCO & 15 men
Cpl Lovick & Cpl Thorne transferred to 3rd Coy
Calais.

Sent to Lorries to Etaples to exchange
23050 rounds "U" Anti SAA & to draw
127000 rounds SAA extra.

Issue 75000 rounds SAA "B" Anti to
6th D.G. for machine gun detachment.
Issue 41000 SAA to Anti Colum & draw
same + 6 boxes Webley pistol amfrom Etaples
2000 rounds SAA to 20th Hussars by car.

18ᵗʰ September Saturday
Fort Rouge

Orderly officer M.S.M. Hardy.
O/c A.S.C. Section. 4850/276/14-9-15 received
by post today. C/1869 L/Cpl Jackman due for
discharge 1-10-15 & has to proceed to Aldershot
at once — Wire sent to Records on 14ᵗʰ No 159
asking for date —
Report to AA & QMG. that all 'U' Amn in Div
has been exchanged for Saa other than B. No of
rounds. 25550 — see 152./78 —
Returns made out & sent in —
Unic Car sent to 2ⁿᵈ Field Squadron —

Petrol consumption made up —
Lorries 155 gall used — 850 miles run
   5.55 miles per gall

Cars. 48 galls used 907 miles run
   18.89 miles per gall

Daimler Car 1910 — over 20 miles per gall
   great improvement.

19th September Sunday
Fort Rouge

Orderly Officer Capt Howard –
Billeting return prepared –
Order came in to exchange all HE given for HE 44/80. Send lorries to Steenzeele & draw 1200 rounds.
Ant. Column asks for 48 rounds Shrapnel after mid-day. These are sent up & drawn from Railhead –
Capt Goldsmith sent to bed by R A M C officer at 11 a.m. poisoned from eating something –
Ant. Return not sent in till asked for at 7. P.M –

20th September Monday -
Fort Rouge
Orderly officer Lieut- Rubery -
One lorry with 174 rounds to J. Battery -
7 rounds to D & 1019 rounds HE 44/80
to Column. J still wants 105 rounds more
to be exchanged -
No more HE 44/80 at Strazeele -
Send lorry to Bethune to draw 1000 hand
bombs. Lorry returns with 2000 as wire
received there from a.a. & d M.G. asking for
2000 while lorry was there -

21st September Tuesday,
Ft Rouge

Orderly Officer Lieut Nesbitt
Left the Park at 7.30 am
Capt Caldwell to no 18 M.G. at 7.30 am
188 H.E. 14 4/50 drawn from Steenzule —
One lorry to R.E. 2nd Field Squadron — Lorry returns
empty.
Instructions received in case of move —
I am not to fill up with extra S.aa viz
243 000 carried on the Horse until units begin
to draw and rounds then complete the Park
to 690 000 rounds.
Units concentrating South — Park to be under
orders of 2nd Cav Div until I hear to the contrary —

Wednesday 28th September –
Fort Rouge

Orderly officer Lieut Rubury –
Fatigue party at 9.30 am –
Capt Alderson to AO + DMC at 7.30 am. Orders to see
Brigade re exchange of B" Amn. + ask if
Regts want the two new limbers arriving in a
day or two loaded with S.A.A. + amounts –
3rd Brigade require 72.000 SAA & 5th Brigade
108.000 SAA. 4th Bty don't require any. re limbers –
3rd Brigade require 160 Return Bombs
tomorrow + 4th Bty 120 per regt –
Deliver 84 13 pr H.E. 44/80 to Amn. Column in
exchange + also 105 to J.Y. Battery. Collect
6 bad rounds from Colum Amn "B" - "D" –
3rd C.D. AC arrive with 48 rounds 13pr Shrapnel
no instructions, so, as I am full, returned them –
Lt Mallows examining all H.E. doubtful

23rd September Thursday.
                                    Fort Rixa

Orderly Officer   Lieut Nisbet.
Cool fatigue at 7.30 a.m.
Capt Goldsmith to O.C - 2 N.C. & then Dr Peel? Joined
Capt Howard with 5 lorries with Bombs Returned
+ 200 for exchange with B & 42 rounds
13 pr HE 44/80 for exchange with same with
Artly Column — 6 good rounds Shrapnel
taken to Column.
Mallows goes to Steazule at 2.P.M. with
two lorries & draws £ 161,000 rounds SAA
+ hands in all time pellets from HE 13pr—
for the Division. Authority O.C. R.H.A 2nd Div.

24th September Friday
Fort Rouge

Orderly Officer M.S. M Hardy.

Capt Goldsmith to AA + QMG at 8.30 am. Park to move to Aire on 26th arrange with Town Major. & report to Car Corps. AA + QMG Signals. Place & time of arrival in billets.

180 rds S.a.a. sent to Aire at 10 am to fill Regtl limbers arriving. All "B" sent to Thiozeele + Park completed with S.a.a.

Car Corps order that 352 rounds 13 pr H.E. gun how with Column can be replaced by the Park with Shrapnel. Lorry leaves at 7 pm.

Drew 5000 Francs from Pay Master.

Coal fatigue party at 7 am.

Make White & Stephen L/Cpls. Send White to Amm. Column.

Pte Neilson up for driving a lorry too fast — Forfeits 4 days pay.

Go & see Town Major at AIRE. Sent on to D.A. Q.M.G. 1st Army arrange to Billet at BOESEGHEM

25th September Saturday.

Fort Rouge

Orderly Officer Capt Howard —

Captain Goldsmith to Hd Qrs. moved to Monchy-Cayeux.
to report move of Park & where I was going to Billet.
See OC. Amn Column & arrange the system of
orderlies —

Send in to Claims of Damage from billets one for
workshop 25 Francs; the other cook House 35 Francs —

Send in returns report destination of Park to
Cav. Corps & Signals —

Vauxhall Car 1786 — damaged — Lt. Rubury driving
caused by hub-cap of lorry protruding beyond wings —
Damage — Dumb iron off side badly bent & broken
showed signs of having been broken for a long
time —

Hd Qrs moved to
Send orderly to Hd Qrs for letters etc —

Making out billeting return up to & including
tonight & get them signed by Mayor.

The 352 rounds HE gun exchanged with
column for shrapnel can be exchanged
at railhead for shrapnel —

26th September Sunday.
              Fort Rouge to Boeseghem.
Orderly Officer Lieut Rodney.
Park moves off at 8:30 am & arrives
at Boeseghem at 9-45 am. Fix up billets
cook-House, workshops. & Latrines.
Send orderly to find signal office.
Make out billeting return for Ammn & send
it in with Billeting return to Anc.
Head Quarters at LOZINGHEM
Lorry 3029 burnt out its clutch leather on
the journey.
One lorry to Strazeele to draw 168 Ball grenades
complete. 80 grenades Hand No-6. Complete
48 grenades hand No-5.   Complete.
to be carried on Park.
Ordered to take off all 2o Cas Div. & Ammn Park from
lorries & to paint ▨▨▨▨ in red 6" × 14"

on both sides of lorries.

Start on cleaning off old name.

27th September Monday.
Boesegheu

Orderly officer Lieut Nisbet —
Orderly firm column arrives Heavy Echelon in the
same place — 13pr am'n can be drawn from
LAPUGNOY —
10.30 a.m. wire comes in to say Maire car with 2nd
Field Squadron broken down ½ mile N. W. of MARLES
LES - MINES at level crossing — send Nisbet out to tow in
Lt Nisbet repaired Maire car which returned
to Park at 8 P.M. —
No HE 44/80 available for exchange either at
Strazule or Lapugnoy —
Letter comes in from Am'n Column asking for
another motor cyclist as O.C R.H.A. has ordered
the one with Heavy Section to go to the Light Section
write to AA & QMG + complain of O.C R.H.A. ordering
my men about —

28th September Tuesday
BOESEGHEM

Orderly Officer M.S.M. Hardy.
Capt. Goldsmith to AA+QMG at 8am. re cycle orderlies. Matter cleared up. The cycle orderly to live with light echelon & to go through Heavy to Park. All cars to return to Park.
No HE 44/80 available for exchange.
Daimler Car No 1910 returns to Park.
Visit Westrehem as Park will move there in case of a move.
Heavy echelon to FERFAY.
All traffic on road LABUISSIÈRE - NOEUX-Les-MINES - MAZINGARBE to go east only.
Ordnance stores arrive files & twist drills etc.
Duties of RA + ASC officer on Park laid down G.R.O. 1172.

29th September Wednesday
                                Boesegheim
Orderly officer Capt. Howard
Lorry 6088 to Steazeele to be refiled near
here & to draw 6000 rounds SAA
C/1907 Pte Hanna G. to England for discharge
on the 15-10-15.
Lieut Mallows to Steazeele Lapugnoy & Column
ho HE 44/80 for exchange.
Heavy Echelon and Column to ESTREE-
BLANCHE.
Div. Head Quarters to AUCHY-au-BOIS.
Sent five Bills to DAD. for communication
total amount 75.60 Francs.

Petrol consumption made up
Lorries 240 galls used 1304 miles run
    5.43 miles per gall.

30th September Thursday.
BOESEGHEM –

Orderly Officer Lieut Rubery –
Lieut Mallows to Steenjule + Amm Column –
Amm Column to ENQUIN-les-MINES &
Div Head Quarters to ECQUEDECQUES –
Testimonials for the wife of Sergt Randall returned
from O/c ase Base –
M.T. Stores sent up. deficient on one voucher
Return of Motor Cars & Motor Cycles.
Have to send in return showing amount of
glycerine required – Estimate 62 galls first issue
& 16 galls per week normal times –

Local order all Estaminet to be closed at
8.P.M. give orders to that effect.

G.L. Goldsmith Capt
A.S.C
OC 2nd Cav Div Amm Park

3rd October 1915

2nd Cavalry Sworn

2/7368

2nd Lieut. Scott answer in

Fort Ellis

Oct. 15

1st October Friday -
                    Boeseghem -
Orderly officer Lieut Nisbet -
One brigade 21st Division - billeted in this area -
As I am in the 1st Army area I have to give way
only billet to be given up is my own -

Lieut Mallows to Strazeele + Amb. Column
at ENQUIN - Les - MINES.

Lieut Rubury test run on M.1697. leather drive
requires repair - Purchase the leather; as
it is an M.T. supply requires authority
from a D of S+T -

Value of 5 francs is 3/7 for October -

2nd October Saturday
Boeseghem

Orderly Officer M.S.M Hardy.
Capt Goldsmith to aa&QMG at 8 a.m.
To report on road to Villers au Bois – return
at 2.30.a.m. As soon as cars are repaired
send one to o.c R.H.a. Vauxhall 1786.M –
steering arm broken.
172 rounds 13pr HE faire exchanged for
44/80 at Strazeele.
Returns sent in –
7 Ball bombs found in the Billets evacuated
by the 21st Division –
Pte Bladen. C 10th foot Regt reports at 8.P.M.
21st Div marched out at 8.30.a.m

Unic Car in shops for leather drive broken –

Vauxhall 1786. in shops broken steering
arm. new one requires to be made –

3rd October Sunday.
Boeseghem

Orderly Officer Capt Howard
Send Diary for September to D.A.G Base
Amm. Return sent in. 172 rounds HE 114/80
1396 rounds HE gain & 1132 Shrapnel.
1000 Bethune Bombs drawn.
For week ending 1-10-15 - Miles per gall for
lorries 4.56 - 155½ galls petrol for 710 miles
very low owing to 3029 & 3041 doing so
badly. Cars 37½ galls to 670 miles
average 17.86 m.p.g.
5527 using a lot of lubricating oil, explanation
asked for.
Schedule of supplies for week sent in.

Adv. Div. H.Qrs moved to HAM. en ARTOIS.

4th October Monday.
Boeseghem

Orderly officer Lieut Rubury

Send imprest acc. away. Balance due to paymaster 237.30 francs.

No Y/586 Pte Burke to England for discharge.

Ask for covering authority for the purchase of 8 francs worth of leather for Unic Car.

Lorry 3029 + 3041 out on test run of two galls. average 10.4 + 9.6 miles per two galls.

Billeting certificate to a.o + a M.G. 88.00 francs. Interpret includes from 1st October (2 nights).

5th October Tuesday.
Boeseghem

Orderly officer Lieut Nisbet.
T4/085750 Pte Hopper A. 8 days No 1 Field Pun
for absent from 7.30 am till 11.30 am 4th inst.
Unic Car M.1697 sent to OC R.Ha.
Vauxhall Car M.1786 out of shops.
Lieut Mallows draws 24 Detonators
No 8 with 2' safety fuze from Shazule.

6th October Wednesday.
                    Boesinghen

Orderly Officer M.S.M Hardy.
Capt Goldsmith to a.a + q.m.g.
Capt Goldsmith on special leave to England for 72 hrs
Lieut Mallows drawn issues to
4th Hussars, 5th Lancers 16th Lancers
2 boxes each Rifle grenades — & 1 box
detonators No. 8. with 2ft safety fuze for
5th Lancers.

7th October Thursday.
                    Boesinghen
Orderly Officer Lieut Rubury –
Vauxhall Car M.1786 lent to AO&D M.G.
to report at NEDON at 9.0 am returned to
Park at 8.30 p.m.
Lieut Mallows to St Razeele + Antè Column
draws 1104 rounds Pistol Webley –
1000 Detonators for Bethune Bombs drawn
from 2d Field Squadron –

8th October Friday.
Bolenghum

Orderly officer Lieut Nisbet.

Capt Howards draws 6000 francs & pays out the company.

Lieut Mallows to Strazule & An.t Column

OC 2nd Field Squadron handed over bomb carriers. Unic Car M1697 handed over from OC R.H.A to OC 2nd Field Squadron

One lorry to AIRE to collect four spare gun wheels.

9th October Saturday.
Boesinghem

Orderly Officer M.S.M Hardy.
Returns sent in — Petrol book made up.
Capt Goldsmith returns from leave.

Lorries run in week 220 — 65½ galls used
3.36 miles per gall. 14½ galls used by lorries
not going out miles 4.31. Very bad owing to
small mileage done.

Order all lorries to go out next week.

Cars 60 galls used for 962 miles average
16.03 m.p.g.

10th October Sunday
Boesegheur

Orderly Officer Capt. Howard.
Church parade at 9.15 a.m.
Receive a receipt voucher from Base for stores sent down.
Lent Mallows to Strazeele.
One lorry to Strazeele to draw 396 Grenades Hand Mills No.1. & 155 grenades rifle.

One lorry issue. 4th Brigade. 8 boxes Bethune bombs. 13 boxes detonators.

3rd Brigade 5 boxes bombs Bethune & 8 boxes Detonat
5th   "   8   "   "   "   & 13   "   "
& 3 boxes SAA for Oxford Hussars.

11th October Monday.
                    Boiseghem
Orderly officer Lieut Rubury.
Vauxhall Car M 1786 sent to St Omer for
repair. Frame between radiator & spring bracket
broken. On 21st Sept Lt Rubury had slight accident
frame repaired but will not stand.
Report to ADofS&T, AA & QMG.
One lorry to Bethune for 1000 bombs
One lorry to units to issue 96 Ball Bombs
to units & 36 grenades No 5. Mills to units
also 40 Rifle grenades to Oxfords, Scots Greys
12th Lancers & 3rd & 20th Hussars. 13000
rounds SAA & 1 bom woollen to Amn Column
Send Billeting return to AA & QMG
Receipt for Car sent back but no receipt
for tools etc promised to be sent next day —

12th October ~~Wednesday~~ Tuesday

Boeseghem

Orderly Officer Lieut Nisbet.

Capt Goldsmith to AA & QMG at 8.30 am
One lorry with 137 Grenades hand mills
No. 1 to each Brigade i.e. 44 per unit
+ 360 Bethune Bombs to 3rd Brigade
13000 S.A.A to Austln Colm + 1 box revolver
The explosives handed in by Scots Greys
surplus to their requirements, they only
want rifle grenades to complete them —

Lieut Mallows to Steenjecle draws 1 box of
Webley Pistol ammn. to 2nd Field Squadron
+ draws 1000 detonators for Bethune Bombs.

Pte Wheeling reported absent; report received
from No. 6 G.H.Q. Austln Park that he is under
arrest in their guard room. Send escort.

13th October Wednesday.
                                    Boesinghem
Orderly officer M.S.M. Hardy.

Send to O/c A.S.C. Section Base A.F.W. 3125 for Vasey, Mason, White, Wright, Wickens, Harland & Grierson.

Pte Wheeling forfeits 4 days Pay, for not reporting to NCO i/c picquet on leaving Park & absent.

14th October Thursday.
                                    Boesinghem
Orderly officer Captain Howard.

Draw 1000 Bethune Bombs.

Issue to Amtn Column 10000 rounds S.a.a. + 4 boxes Webley. Two wheels No 457.

Lieut Mellows to Steenzeele.

16th October 1915. Friday.
                                Boeseghem

Orderly Officer Lieut Rubury.
Capt Goldsmith & Lt. hallows to Itéogule to
draw 12 Cylinders No. 120 _ 12 boxes matches
Vesuvian _ 25 Detonators electric No 13 _
100 yds Fuze Instantaneous & issue as detailed
One lorry to St Venant to draw 1008 Grenades
No 5. Mills & 1008 Grenades Ball _ For
instructional purposes. Allowed to keep Ball
Bombs. Prepare slates etc _
No detonators with Bethune Bombs.
3 Ton lorry will carry 4000 Bethune Bombs
or 2400 Ball bombs.

16th October Saturday.
Orderly officer Lieut Nisbet.   Boesughem
Draw 1656 Grenades Ball complete.
Issue to units 2664 Ball bombs.
Make out mileage —
Lorries 192½ galls used 1015 miles run
average 5.27 m p g.

17th October Sunday.
Orderly officer M.S.M Hardy.   Boesughem
Church Parade at 9. a.m.
Capt. Goldsmith draws 6650 Francs
Division on the move H! Qrs at Requetoire
at 12.30 mid day.

18th October Monday.

Boesinghem

Orderly Officer Capt Howard.

Capt Goldsmith & 2/Lt Ejos sent to report on two villages as a Park for the lorries they are not suitable but can just get in.

Following men go on 6 months leave. Sgt Vasey L/Cpl White. Cpl Wright. Ptes Harland. Mason Greirson & Cpl Wickens —

One lorry & O.C. Signals to parade at 6 a.m. will be away 18th 19th 20th & 21st.

2/Lt Heslet pays out the men going on leave

Pte Coles takes over duties of cycle orderly with Anti Column in place of L/Cpl White —

19th October Tuesday.
                    Boeseghem
Orderly officer Lt Rubury.
One lorry to Calais for AOD stores order aardvee.
Leaves at 6 am.
Billeting Return sent to AA & QMG signed by the Mayor.

20th October Wednesday.
                    Boeseghem
Orderly officer Lt Nisbet.
Receive Warrant Book for NCo's & men
 A 65901 to A 66600 — also Warrant Book
for Officers A. 38001 to A 38100 —
Lt Nisbet pays out not enough pay for the RHA
Lt Nisbet to Repair shops at St Omer to
see about repair of hood for Mice Car
No 1697.
Lt Mallows draws 96 charges wet gun cotton
from Strazeele & issues it —
Instructions re Smoke Helmets issued
to all the men —

21st October Thursday.
Boesyghem.
Orderly Officer M.S.M. Hardy.
"Q" office moved to THIEMBRONNE.
Lieut Mallows R.F.A. ordered to 20th Division when relief arrives. Car sent to H.Q. for Major Clinch.

22nd October Friday.
Boesyghem
Orderly Officer Capt Howard.
Capt. Howard takes out his section on test run. Gunner Brown on leave.
All S.A.A. examined for "W" manufacture none in Park.
Lieut Rubury & Lieut Mallows on leave.

L: Mallows draws 132 Mills No 5.

23rd October Saturday.
Boesynhem
Orderly officer Lieut Nisbet -
Capt Goldsmith to Strazeele to draw 25 electric
detonators. 1000 rounds SAA & 12 bomens
matches - Capt Howard issued them in
the afternoon to 2nd Field squadron -
Returns & states sent in. Signed by Capt
Howard - Issued 132 hills No 6 & 2 - 7.1

24th Sunday
Boesynhem
Orderly officer M.S.M. Hardy.
Major Goldsmith to AA & Q M G at 8.30 am
Billeting return sent in -

Pte. Hacquet sent to England yesterday due
for discharge on 7th November -

2 Lieut E. Gildon arrived last night & taken to
H. Qrs. Go to see 2nd Field Squadron
re Block lights for Bethune bombs -
Officers & men have been sent on leave
a day too soon. D. Rubury ordered detailed
as officer i/c men going on leave from 2nd
Car Div -

26th October Monday

Orderly Officer Capt Howard — Boeseghem

Take Mess Car M1697 into repair shops St
Omer to have Hood repaired also mud wings.
One lorry to Bethune to draw 1500 Bombs.
Lt Gildon draws 4000 S.a.a & 1 box revolver
from Stogule & issues to Amm Column
Amm Column send in 3 Boxes "W" ammn
6 Boxes matches Vesuvian drawn from Stogule
16 Boxes S.a.a. issued to 3rd Hussars.
Send instructions to Lieut Rubury detailing him
as O/c men returning from leave on the
29th. Report arrival of Lt Gildon R.F.A

26th October Tuesday.

Orderly Officer Lieut Nisbet - Boesyhem
Capt Howard inspects Smoke Helmets.
Gunners White & Phillips absent from 6.30 a.m. 26th inst.
Order a daily roll call at 8.15 P.M. under orderly officer.

Lieut Gildon to Hazule for 3 bores revolver & to take 3 bores W. anti
Then to Field Squadron as there are no Block lighters for Bethune Bombs to be had at St Venant

Issue 500 Bethune Bombs to each Brigade & have to use lighters from my reserve - 15 20 short.

Two bores W. Anti S.A. received from 4th Brigade H! Qrs.

One lorry to O.C. Signals to remain there till 28th inst.

27th October Wednesday.
                    Boesegham

Orderly Officer M.S.M. Hardy.
Car to be at J Battery at 10. a.m. to take Capt
Loammi to 14th Div. Hd Qrs.

Major Goldsmith to AA+QMG. at 1 P.M.
Arrange to send 6 lorries to 2nd Field Squadron
for trench digging work.

            28th October Thursday.
                    Boesegham

Orderly Officer Capt. Howard.
5 lorries only to 2nd Field Squadron one still
with Signals. OC to AA+QMG at 8.30am
Draw 6000 francs.
Arrange to take up 800 pairs dungaree trousers
to 2nd Field Squadron.

Lend Car to D.O.O. for the afternoon.

29th October Friday.
                    Boeseghem
Orderly officer Lieut Nisbet.
M.S.M. Hardy - Sergt Randall, Sergt Bushell
& Sergt Molineux to Havre on way to England
for duty with new army.

Unic Car returns from G.H.Q. repair shops.

Lieut Rubrey & Lieut Mallows return from leave

            30th October Saturday.
                        Boeseghem
Orderly officer Capt Howard.
Returns sent in - AF B 213 checked with
nominal roll. Found correct.
No Brock lighters available anywhere
report to Div Bomb officer.
Lieut Mallows R.F.A. to 20th Division for
duty.

31st October Sunday.
                    Boeseghem

Orderly officer Lieut Rubury –
Receive 8 new passes –
Pay out the Company –
Billeting return sent to Mayor for signature
total amount 107.65 francs.

Captain Howard on leave starting at 2.15 P.M,
at 6.0 P.M. an orderly arrived with 8.31 –

Not opened till 8 P.M. found that leave could
not be granted. Too late to take action –

Daimler M 1910 – skidded into ditch & broke
Hood & wind screen.
L. Gilson drew 1500 Detonators No. 8. Mark VII
1500 fuze lighters. 72 ft soft fuze No 10.

                G. R. Goldsmith Major
                                     a/c

        O.C. 2 Coy Div Auto Park

1-11-15.

2nd Cavalry Division 2/Cav. Amm. Pk.

Nov.
Vol XLV

121/7655

O.t
056

1st November Monday.
                                Boeseghem
Orderly Officer Lieut Nisbet.
Diary for October sent to D.A's Base.
One lorry to Bethune to draw 1500 Bombs.
No Brock lights available. Sent Gildon down
Detonators etc yesterday.
Report departure of 2Lt. W.A. Mallows R.F.a.
Issue new passes and send back all
old passes.
Send Bills to D.D.O. for countersignature
6 Bills total, 140.50 Francs.

Send Billeting return to AA+Q.M.G

2ⁿᵈ November Tuesday.
                    Boeseghem
Orderly Officer Lt Rutsey.
Major Goldsmith to Hd Qrs.

Lorry issues 500 Bombs to each unit. Brigade
Hd Qrs.

3ʳᵈ November Wednesday.
                    Boeseghem.
Orderly Officer Lt Nisbet.
Daimler Car 1910 to Repair depot
St Omer. Cpl Howard + 6 men absent
from roll call at 8.15 P.m. 2=
Extra guards for men + Cpl Howard upieus

Ptᵉ Geddes + Ptᵉ McDougall on leave.

Meerhut Division billeted in Boeseghem
area. Order arrived for me to move early
next morning at 11.30 P.m.

4th November Thursday.
DESVRES

Orderly Officer Lt Rubury.
Park moves to DESVRES. Have to make
drains as been mud + wet off.
Major Goldsmith with ADOS DAS + ANC.
Hand priest pass to O.P.M.

5th November Friday
DESVRES

Orderly officer Lt Nisbet.
No Beer in the village so start a wet
canteen.
AA + QMG arrives at 3.30 P.m. till
him I can order bricks for standings
for lorries + ashes. Also suggest using
workshop to light barn used as men's
dining room.

8th Nov. Monday.
DESURES.

~~It list~~ orderly officer – Lt Rubery.
Major Goldsmith on leave, leaves at 9.30
am for Boulogne – Capt Howard to 2nd F.S.
for wood for revetting ditches on side of road
One lorry to Bethune for 1500 Bombs.
Car returns at 2.30 pm

9th November Tuesday
DESURES

Orderly officer Lt Nisbet.
~~Draw~~ 6000 Francs.
Lorry issues Bombs 500 to each Brigade H.Qs
Lt Rubery takes lorries to draw wood
Lorry No 2160 to replace No 3041 – at 2nd F.S
owing to break down.
Vauxhall to 1st Army for Canteen Stores.

10th November Wednesday
BESVRES

Orderly Officer Lieut Pubrey.
Paid 'out' the Company.
Lt Gildon to Stiazule for detonators
Lorry to Stiazule for 60.000 rounds 3aa
& 7 Boxes revolver.
Recievd orders to stop all winter constructional
work as billets likely to be altered.

11th November Thursday
BESVRES

Orderly Officer Lieut Nisbet.
Lt Gildon appointed to inspect all explosives
in Division.
Capt Howard to AA & MG to ask for Sunbeam
from 2nd Field Squadron. Not granted
then to AD of H.T. re car to replace Daimler

Lorry to Wardrecque for Coal & to pick
up coke on its return journey at Aire

12th November Friday
BEOVRES

Orderly officer Lieut Rubury.
Lt Gilson out all day in Vauxhall to inspect explosives of 3rd + 4th Brigades.
Two men on leave.
No car left on Park for OC Park.
New billeting area allotted.

13th Nov Saturday
Beovres

Orderly Officer Lieut Nisbet.
Lt Gilson to inspect explosives of 5th Cav Brigade. All returns sent in
ADOS Sgt arrived at Park but only left a message that Major Goldsmith was to attend at Director of Requisition Services Office as soon as he returns from leave

14th Nov. Sunday.
                    Besores
Orderly Officer Lt. Rubury.
Lorry to Strazeele to draw Miller hand
grenades & 1500 brock lighters —
Billeting return made out.

15th November Monday
                    Besvres
Orderly officer Lt. Nisbet.
Lorry to Bethune to draw 1500 Bombs
then issue to Brigades. 4th Brigade only
brigade who took them others refused on
account of move.
Park ordered to DRIONVILLE Capt. Howard
went there & found it impossible for the Park
reported to d.a. + d. M.G.
Pte Honeygold Transferred to 1st Bt. Middlesex
Regt.
Later was ordered to report on CRHEM.

16th Nov. Tuesday.
                    Besures.
Orderly Officer Lt. Rubury.
Capt Howard to CREHEM _ it is impossible for the Park. report to AA & QMG sanction given for Park to go to AVROULT not in Cav Corps area.
Major Goldsmith returns from leave.

17th November Wednesday.
                    Besures to AVROULT.

Orderly Officer Lieut Nisbet.
Major Goldsmith & Interpreter Paulmier to office of D of Requi: Services re motor car requisitioned by Major Hay RFA on 31st August 1914.
Park moves to AVROULT _ arrives at 3.30 P.M. Billeting return for BESURES sent in _ signed by Mayor.

18th Nov. Thursday.
AVROULT.

Orderly officer Captain Howard
Lt Gildon to Hazuele in Vauxhall
Major Goldsmith to AA+QMG at 11-45am
OC ASC arrived about 3 P.m.

19th Nov Friday
AVROULT.

Orderly officer Lt Rubury
Lt Nisbet on leave, till 29th Nov. goes
down in Vauxhall. 6 RFA to Wardrecque
for coal fatigue for a week rations to 20th
Wolseley Car M. 1470 received from OC
ASC 1st Cav Div report arrival by wire
to ADof S.+T. + to OC ASC 1st Cav Div

20th November Saturday
AVROULT.

Orderly Officer Capt Howard.
Lt Gildon to Strazeele to inspect fuzes? & collect 1500 Brock lighters in Wolseley. Wolseley broken down.

Send in all returns. Men on 1 months leave return except 1 Cpl White who is not fit for active service & sent to Aldershot.

21st November Sunday
AVROULT.

Orderly Officer Lt Rubring
Wolseley Car requires a complete overhaul
Lt Gildon to E Battery to examine fuzes & then to Strazeele. No Brock lighters available. Unic Car fit for the road again.

Fix up workshop lorry to meet demands for workshop as Douglas engine failed.

22nd November Monday.
                    AVROULT.
Orderly Officer Captain Howard.
Start teaching NCO semaphore.
Lorry to Bethune to draw 1500 Bombs
Lorry 3341 to Hazebrouck to be refitted both front
wheels.
Lorry arrives from GHQ to be repaired
in Park workshops.

            23rd November Tuesday
                    AVROULT
Orderly Officer Lt Rubury.
Vauxhall car requires back brakes to be
relined.
Lorry issues Bombs to Brigade HQ. Etc
+ to Boxes Vesuvian matches to 3rd Cav
Brigade.
Orders received for Major Goldsmith to
go to SARTON to take over command of
4th Div Supply Column.

November 22nd 1915
AVROULT

Orderly Officer Captain Howard –

Major Goldsmith & Captain Howard visited A.A. & Q.M.G. 4th Division – The A.D. of S&T and D.A. & Q.M.G. Cav Corps –

Major Goldsmith, handed over company to Captain Howard –

Vauxhall repairs completed.

D.A.D of S&T orders report to be sent in re Wolsey Car No 1470

November 25th 1915 AVROULT

Major Goldsmith leaves in Vauxhall for SARTON to take over command of 4th Div Sup Col.

Payed out the men

Received notice to warn M Paulmier to attend a court martial to give evidence, at a court martial at ST OMER at some early date to be notified later.

November 26th 1915 Friday

AVROULT

Orderly Officer Lieut Rubury.
2nd Lieut Geldon To STRAZEEL for lighters which he was unable to obtain
Report on Wolsey Car sent in to the A.D. of S&T.

November 27th 1915 Saturday
AVROULT

Orderly Officer Lieut Rubury.
2nd Lieut Geldon went on leave
Sent in all returns
Party of 6 men for coal at WARDECQUES relieved & another 6 sent in their place.
M Paulmier warned to attend Court Martial at ST OMER on November 29th.

November 28th 1915
AVROULT

Orderly Officer Lieut Rubury

Received orders from the A.A.D. 2 W.G. that the Heavy Section (Lorries with 13 pr) were to go on detachment to the 1st Army.

Visited A.A.D 2 m G to make arrangements then reported myself to the O.C.A.S.C. and informed him of the arrangements made.

Arranged with the Supply officer to ration the men on detachment up to & including Dec 1st

Arranged for 8 Lorries under Lt Rubury to go to 46 A.S.P. at St VENANT and three lorries to No 7 A.S.P. under a Sergeant

Lt Rubury went in the lorries and interviewed the Officers Commanding Nos 7 & 46 A.S. Parks and made all necessary arrangements with these officers.

Lieut Nesbit returned off leave.

Paid out men who had been on detachment with 2nd Field Squadron R.E.

Asked Senior Supply Officer for the return of the 6 men from WARDRECQUES

November 29th 1915 Monday

AVROULT

Sunbeam towed in from 2nd F.S.R.E.
water pump spindle having been broken

Advised of the arrival of 2nd Lt Lucas R.F.A.
on the park.

Forwarded to A.A. & Q.M.G. a report of the
arrangements I had made with regard to
the detachment. Also a return showing
strength & personnel I proposed sending.

Visited by A.A.Q. 2 M G, who approved of
the arrangements made.

O C R H A. called for a report showing
the amount of 13 pr ammunition with
the sub-section detailed to be attached
to No 46 A.S.P. (How much Shrapnel
& how much H E) Report forwarded at once.

Lt Rabury to STRAZEEL to try and
get detonators & fuses for Bethune Bombs
he was able to draw 3000 — Two weeks supply

Lt Nesbit R.F.A. to WIZERNES to fetch 2nd Lt
Lucas who reported his arrival to me at 6.0 pm

Lorry to WARDRECQUES to bring back
the six men from Coal fatigue.

M. Paulmier to St Omer to give evidence at
a Court Martial.

November 30th 1915 Tuesday
Orderly Officer Lieut Nesbit

AVROULT

Party of 1 NCO & 15 men to the gas demonstration at 10.0 a.m.

Lorry out to the 3rd, 4th & 5th Brigade Head Quarters to issue bombs

Lt Ruburg left park with 11 lorries & 46 other ranks to go on detachment to the 1st Army at 12.30 p.m.

3 lorries 1 sergeant & 12 other ranks to No 7. A.S.P.

8 lorries 1 car 1 officer & 32 other ranks to No 46. A.S.P.

Sent Bills to D.O.O. for counter signature three bills total = 36.00 francs

1.12.15

E.W. Howard
Capt A.S.C.
O.C. 2nd Cavalry Division Ammunition Park.

Reference Map. Hazebrook 5A
Scale. 1/80,000.

CONFIDENTIAL.

War Diary

of

2nd Cavalry Division Ammunition Park

to 31st 12/15

Volume 2. No 12
Vol XV

From 1st 12/15

WAR DIARY
or
INTELLIGENCE SUMMARY

Army Form C. 2118

Place	Date	Hour	Summary of Events and Information	Remarks and references to Appendices
AVROULT	1.12.15	10.0 am	Sergt Major sent to Hospital on account of fall off motor bicycle.	
		10.30 am to 12.0 am	Went and saw the A.A.D. of S. of Division Corps but found him out, while I was away the Park was visited by the A.D. of S. & T. Cavalry Corps. Br. NESBIT took him round. He ordered the shell sign to be painted vertical present sign rather thus . Ordered lorries to be repainted, and workshop stores to be more carefully looked after. [Sgd.] H
"	2.12.15	8.45 am to 10.30 am	Went to see the A.D. of S. & T. but found him out - told to go the next day at same time. On return found the D. of T. Inspector was examining the lorries - Found the workshops dirty and others rusty but kept in good order otherwise. Reported remaining lorries to be well kept and in good condition.	
		2.30 pm	Visited by O.C. A.S.C. who went round the Park. Discussed with him details with regard to baths for the men & informing general condition of Park. [Sgd.] H
"	3.12.15	9.30 to 10.30	Visited the A.D. of S. & T. who told me he was not pleased with condition of the Park. I pointed out that I had only taken over the Company five days and that we had been very much in arrangements for the detachment under Jr. RUBURY going away. I told him J. Thetherd he would inspect the Park again when I had had time to get things straight.
		10.30 2.0 pm	2nd Lt Lucas to BOLOGNE to draw 1000 miles for a Gles Mr. Nesbit took up some spare parts for lorries - nails etc. to Lt RUBURY. Inspection satisfactory all the men medically examined. [Sgd.] H

Army Form C. 2118

WAR DIARY
or
INTELLIGENCE SUMMARY
(Erase heading not required.)

Instructions regarding War Diaries and Intelligence Summaries are contained in F. S. Regs., Part II. and the Staff Manual respectively. Title Pages will be prepared in manuscript.

Place	Date	Hour	Summary of Events and Information	Remarks and references to Appendices
AVROULT	4.12.15	—	Sent in all returns for week ending Dec 4th. Forwarded my Inspect Account for November 1915 to base. Sergt Hoyt returned from Hospital.	
		9.30am	Pte Shuttler sent for by D.A. & V.M.G. Car Corps. re his Application for un intetranster.	
		10.30am	Milk tombs issued 100 to each regiment & 150 to Parks	1036K
"	5.12.15	9.0am	Pte Hamilton, who saw an attachment shot not appear in list to get L.O.A.P. on & lcut This morning	
		8.0am	Car to BOULOGNE to draw Practice ammunition with lorry; afterwards lorry delivered ammunition to Ex Houtroux	Yesterday
			Lorry to BETHUNE for tombs.	
		9.30am	Visited O.C.A.S.C. & A.A.&Q.M.G. of the Division.	
			Ordered Lt NESBIT to take stock of workshop stores. & made arrangements for baths & bath room for the men.	1036K
"	6.12.15		Sent in Ammunition return to him.	
		2.0pm	Lt Nabit to St VENANT to take mails off to attachment. No lorries out. Today.	1036K
"	7.12.15	8.0am	Lorry issued tombs to Brigade head-quarters.	
		2.0pm	Lt NESBIT & M.PAUMIER (interpreter) to St OMER to purchase wood. Received a notification that the totablishment of the Regiments colonies & parks were to be altered in smalls Amn Ammunition and also they were to carry a certain fixed number of Mills No 5 Grenades — all This is to be adjusted by the Parks	1036K

1875 Wt. W593/826 1,000,000 4/15 J.B.C. & A. A.D.S.S./Forms/C. 2118.

WAR DIARY
or
INTELLIGENCE SUMMARY

(Erase heading not required.)

Army Form C. 2118

Place	Date	Hour	Summary of Events and Information	Remarks and references to Appendices
AVROULT	8.12.15		2/Lt GILDON, R.F.A. returned off leave - Notified him that he was to proceed to the 1st Div: Brigade R.F.A. Hd Qrs. to report thereto for duty - 2nd Lt GILDON handed over officially to 2nd Lt LUCAS R.F.A.	
		2.0 pm	They went to ST VENANT to hand over -	
		3.0 pm	A.A. & 2.M.G. inspected Park - seemed cleaner & satisfied. Procured ways & means of ordinary ventilation of S.A.A. & Bombs - (Vide my entry of the 7th inst.)	
"	9.12.15		Received urgent message for another car from Lt RUBURY at ST VENANT. Sent Lt GILDON to 17th Division in Sanctuary Wood after dropping him proceeded to join Lt RUBURY at ST VENANT	
		9.0 am 9.30 am	Lorry to ESTRE-BLANCHE for stores - harbouring ground for lorries being very soft 2nd Lt LUCAS inspected the influence stores of the regiments of the 3rd Cavalry Brigade in the afternoon	
"	10.12.15	8.0 am 8.30 am	Lorry adjusted S.A.A. of the 5th Cavalry Brigade Regiments - (Vide my entry of the 7th inst.) Lorry for stores to ESTRE-BLANCHE Lt Lucas inspected the influence stores of the 3rd & 4th Brigades' regiments	
		11.0 am	2nd Lt E.K.D. ROACH, A.S.C. reported for duty from No. 4 G.H.Q. Park	
"	11.12.15		Sent in the weekly returns	
		9.0 am	Went into BOULOGNE & interviewed C.O.O there and (1) obtained authority to thumb surplus ammunition extraction from units on account of rehabilitation (Vide entry of 7th inst.) (2) Drew requisition & fuses for Bethune bombs (3) Arranged to draw 6,500 balls No 5 grenades required to complete the total ammunition establishment	
		3.0 am	Received Lt RUBURY's diary & return for lorries on detachment - Sorry to regiment of 3rd Cav. Brigade to make the necessary adjustments in S.A.A. (Vide entry of 7th inst.) Adjustment for S.A.A. in the Divisional Cavalry Est. - Notified A.A. & Q.M.G. of the fact.	

WAR DIARY
or
INTELLIGENCE SUMMARY
(Erase heading not required.)

Army Form C. 2118

Instructions regarding War Diaries and Intelligence Summaries are contained in F.S. Regs., Part II. and the Staff Manual respectively. Title Pages will be prepared in manuscript.

Place	Date	Hour	Summary of Events and Information	Remarks and references to Appendices
AVROULT	12.12.15	8.0 am	Orderly Officer 2/Lt Nesbit. 2nd Lt ROACH took two lorries to BOULOGNE. He claimed 76,100 rounds of S.A.A. and drew 65,000	
			MILLS grenades No 5 required to complete Divisional Establishment.	
		4.30 am	2nd Lt RUBURY came & reported personally from ST VENANT. He took back some spare parts for lorries	
		5.30 am	1st Lt LUCAS R.F.A. went to ST VENANT.	
		8.0 am to 10.30 am	Voluntary church parade in recreation room. After drawing bombs at BOULOGNE raced them to the regiment. Lorries completed with the exception of columns.	
"	13.12.15	8.0 am	Orderly Officer 2nd Lt Roach. Lorry took bombs to Columns - Sent notification to A & B 2 M.G. that issue of Mills grenades was completed.	Vide my entry of 7th inst.
		8.0 am	Lorry to BETHUNE to draw practice bombs. (1500 bombs)	
"	14.12.15	8.0 am	Orderly Officer 2/Lt Nesbit. Lorry to 32 & 8/5th Brigade Head quarters to collect 500 Belteam bands to render for the regiments	
		8.20 am	Senior Supply Officer came round & by 3 Lorries a trip for his Vauxhall - none of right-age in stock.	
		9.0 am	Visits the Cashier and asked for money - He promised to come round the next day	
		11.30 am	Visits D.O.O. refoint for lorries not yet arrived asked to be permitted to purchase locally. Lt Rubury reported all going well at ST VENANT	
"	15.12.15	9.0 am	Orderly Officer 2nd Lt Roach. Sent the Ration lorry to be repaired at HAZEBROUCK. 2/Lt Nesbit to ST OMER to purchase some Mild Steel for workshop. Men had baths	
		4.30 pm	Cashier came and drew 4000 francs	

WAR DIARY
or
INTELLIGENCE SUMMARY
(Erase heading not required.)

Army Form C. 2118

Place	Date	Hour	Summary of Events and Information	Remarks and references to Appendices
AVROULT	16.12.15		2nd Lt Lucas visited Park and came for stores & mails for detachment at ST VENANT.	
		11.0 am	Paid out the men.	
		2.30 pm	Visited by the A.A. to 2 M.g. who asked for our lorries - at a time to be given later - for the transport of the men kit to the trenches. Received an order to purchase paint for lorries.	
"	17.12.15		2nd Lt Roach - Orderly Officer.	
		2.30 pm	Went to St OMER to purchase paint for lorries. Visited dentist about it eventual as I had split one of my teeth in half. No lorries out today.	
"	18.12.15		Lt Nesbit - Orderly Officer: Sent in all the necessary returns for the date. Received orders to return all grenades - not Mills No 5 - to Railhead. Wrote for authority from C.O.D. BOULOGNE to return lorries to Railhead.	
		9.30	Lt Nesbit took lorrie out for a test-run. Magneto lubrication but not quite correct on account of lack of compression.	
			Lt Nesbit drew 2000 francs from the field cashier for imprest account.	
		3.0 pm	Lorrie out & shops to found satisfactory.	

Army Form C. 2118

WAR DIARY
or
INTELLIGENCE SUMMARY
(Erase heading not required.)

Instructions regarding War Diaries and Intelligence Summaries are contained in F.S. Regs., Part II. and the Staff Manual respectively. Title Pages will be prepared in manuscript.

Place	Date	Hour	Summary of Events and Information	Remarks and references to Appendices
AVROULT	19.12.15		2nd Lt. Roach - Orderly Officer.	
		10.30am	Sgt. in Ammunition Dept. returns to Hd. Qrs. A.H.T.Co. Bns. B.I.T. proceeded to Canadian corps Troops Supply Column to obtain gloves sent there in error by A.H.T.Co.	
		11.0am	Inspected all the lorries. H-NES B.I.T. went sick.	
"	20.12.15		H. Nesbit still sick.	
		1.30	Went to see Nesbit for a second visit. Purchasing stores for the Canteen. Wire Car sent to the 2nd Field Squadron R.E.	
"	21.12.15		H. Nesbit letter re sons on light duty.	
		9.0am	Visited A.A. & Q.M.G. about ammunition for Cav. Corps Armoured cars - Sa... 2,000 S.A.A. for them.	
		10.30	H. Rutherby reported that all was correct at S. VENANT. Sent a fresh lorry there had to replace one going to the 5th Cav. Bgde. & returning to withdraw lorries of our D, 2, 9 & K Bgdes for about fortnight.	
		4.30		
"	22.12.15		Sergt. Major went on leave. Nothing of importance occurred during the day.	
"	23.12.15	2.30	Car to S.T. OMER to purchase M.T. stores also to Canteen to buy stuff for men's dinners.	
		3.30	2nd Lt. Tucan arrived from detachment for Clothing for men and to report - all cannot - He in - formed me that the roads round St. VENANT A.H.T. were very bad indeed - was labouring a lot out of the lorries.	

Army Form C. 2118

WAR DIARY
or
INTELLIGENCE SUMMARY
(Erase heading not required.)

Instructions regarding War Diaries and Intelligence Summaries are contained in F. S. Regs., Part II. and the Staff Manual respectively. Title Pages will be prepared in manuscript.

Place	Date	Hour	Summary of Events and Information	Remarks and references to Appendices
AVROULT	24.12.15		Orderly Officer Lt. NISBET. All the men had baths.	
		9.30 am	Lorry to 5th Lancers & 6th Dragoon Guards to issue some Ivoelia Ammunition. Wolsey car finished but not tested.	6/W.H
"	25.12.15		Lt. Roach Orderly Officer. Sent in all returns for the week — Lt Nisbet tested W Olsey car. Christmas Day. General Holiday. Men behaved most on all anxety	6/9.20.H
"	26.12.15		Orderly Officer Lt Nisbet.	
		2.15 h	Church Parade (C of E).	
		2.45 pm	Visited by the O.C. A.S.C. who inspected the park & included my lorries — He found everything in good order — Sent in Ammunition return to A.M.82. M.G.	6/5/6.H
"	27.12.15		Orderly Officer 2/Lt. Roach.	
		9.30 am	Went to BOULOGNE to deliver Bowls withdrawn from the units of the Division; also to draw some S.A.A. required to complete establishment with having ammunition some	vide my entry L.15.12.15 & 21.12.15
		2.30 pm	R.A.A. & S.M.L.E visited park & inquired it all Recruits had been inspected on Dec 12th instant — LOGNE at time — Sent a reply that the Cores completed on	6/7/6.H

1875 Wt. W593/826 1,000,000 4/15 J.B.C. & A. A.D.S.S./Forms/C. 2118.

WAR DIARY
or
INTELLIGENCE SUMMARY

(Erase heading not required.)

Army Form C. 2118

Place	Date	Hour	Summary of Events and Information	Remarks and references to Appendices
AVROULT	28.12.15	2.0 pm	Orderly Officer H. Nickel. Sent a car to ST OMER for medical stores ordered by R.A.M.C. Officer.	
		11.30 am	Received notification of probable return of lorries from 2nd F.S. R.E. Visited O.C. A.S.S. to inquire re: return of acting Corporal (with jaws) to his ranks.	
"	29.12.15	10.30 am	Orderly Officer H. Nichol-wood. Party to collect-wood.	
		2.30 pm	6 lorries on detachment with R.E. arrive back at the Park all apparently in good condition with exception of steering arm of 3638.	
"	30.12.15		Orderly Officer Lt. Roach. Received orders to move on Jan 1st to BOULOGNE to deliver war booty dumped by the 2nd F.S. R.E. — to be relieved up to Jan 3rd	to answer on Jan 12/- to enquiry of 10th & 21st [?]
		12.30	Went to receive instructions from D.A.Q.M.G. Cavalry Corps with reference to drew ration up to & including Jan 3rd with railhead supply Officer	
		6.30 pm	Made arrangements	
"	31.12.15	9.30 am	Orderly Officer Lt. Nickel. Proceeded to BASRIEUX and reported to O.C. 1st Cav. Park found billets- two lorries to each Brigade to collect the mens kits - bedding performed etc. Three of 5's at 5:30 to [?] their tracks to D.A.O.S. dismounted Division at VERQUIGNEUL and returned to park 10:30 pm	
		10.30 am		
		7.30 pm	Made necessary arrangements for move tomorrow.	

[signed] F.W. Hoover
Capt. A.S.C.

O.C. 2nd Cavalry Division Ammunition Park

L of C.

CONFIDENTIAL

WAR DIARY

2nd CAVALRY DIVISION AMMUNITION PARK

From 1/1/16 — To 31/1/16

VOLUME XVI

Army Form C. 2118

WAR DIARY
or
INTELLIGENCE SUMMARY

(Erase heading not required.)

Instructions regarding War Diaries and Intelligence Summaries are contained in F.S. Regs, Part II. and the Staff Manual respectively. Title Pages will be prepared in manuscript.

Place	Date	Hour	Summary of Events and Information	Remarks and references to Appendices
TAILLY (Near LILLIERS) Park situated on the LILLIERS — BETHUNE road $\frac{3}{4}$ of a mile East of cross roads at LOZINGHEM GAS-RIEUX (N.E.) and HAUT-RIEUX (S.W.)	1/1/16	9.00 am 9.30 am 10.0 am 3.45 p.m 5.10 p.m	Sent in all return for week ending Dec 31st. S.A.A. Section moved off under 2nd Lt Roach. One lorry had its radius rod – otherwise uneventful run. Weather very bad – lorries arrived 1.45 p.m. Workshop lorries arrived under Lt. Wisher 2.45 p.m. Transferred 3 lorries with leather jackets etc to VERAVIGNEUL where the loads were taken over by A.D.S. Took in return & reported to O.C. 1st Corps Parks to obtain forms attached.	$\times 2\frac{1}{2}$ miles SSE of BETHUNE [signature]
TAILLY Near LILLIERS	2/1/16	9.30 am 11.30 am 1.30 p.m	Orderly Officer 2nd Lt Roach. Reported to O.C. 1st Corps Parks. Made arrangements to draw supplies with 1st Corps Troops S.C. Sent a lorry to draw Petrol from Railhead.	[signature]
"	3/1/16	9.30 11.30 2.30	Orderly Officer Lt. Wisher. Reporting to O.C. 1st Corps Parks. D.A.D.T.S. Inspector came down to find out what had been done since last report. Found all things reported either in hand & waiting for spare parts or completed. 6 lorries out on Corps work – 30 men went to baths.	[signature]
"	4/1/16	12.30	Orderly Officer 2nd Lt Roach. S Company R.E. Engineers Stores on BETHUNE-VERMELLES road. D.A.D.T.S. Inspector wished further the lorries. Report Feb. Could not be expected to be of any use considering I have had 19 lorries away on various detachments. 2nd Lt Roach to CHOQUES for mail.	[signature]

1875 Wt. W593/826 1,000,000 4/15 J.B.C. & A. A.D.S.S./Forms/C.2118.

Army Form C. 2118

WAR DIARY
or
INTELLIGENCE SUMMARY
(Erase heading not required.)

Instructions regarding War Diaries and Intelligence Summaries are contained in F. S. Regs., Part II. and the Staff Manual respectively. Title Pages will be prepared in manuscript.

Place	Date	Hour	Summary of Events and Information	Remarks and references to Appendices
TAILLY	5.1.16		St Malot - Orderly Officer	
		10.30	Ordered to draw 10,000 Mills No 5 grenades and deliver them to 71 unmounted Div-ision church at VERMELLES - Sent off 2nd Lt Roach with four lorries for the purpose - 2nd Lt Roach got back at 6.45 p.m.	
		11.30		
		12.0	5 lorries for R.E. work to VERMELLES - Returned 8.30 h.m. Visited 1st Corps Troops Supply Column applying for four new motor cycles	WWR
"	6.1.16		2nd Lt. Roach - Orderly Officer	
		12.30	3 lorries out on fatigue duty.	
		2.30 p.m.	O.C. 1st Corps Parks inspected park - found lorries clean - Drew two new motor cycles from S. Rutway joined up to Park	WWR
"	7.1.16		St Michel - Orderly Officer	
		10.30	Two lorries to AUCHEL for gravel & stones for lorry park. Received notification that - all Cavalry ammunition parks were to be put under our Brad. 5 lorries for fatigue duty to R.E.	WWR
"	8.1.16		St Rutway - Orderly Officer.	
		9.0 a.m.	7 lorries out to R.E.	
		11.0 a.m.	Inspected by the A.D. of S. & T Cavalry Corps - Said there was a great improvement on last inspection. Sent in all the necessary returns for the week.	WWR

WAR DIARY
or
INTELLIGENCE SUMMARY
(Erase heading not required.)

Army Form C. 2118

Instructions regarding War Diaries and Intelligence Summaries are contained in F. S. Regs., Part II. and the Staff Manual respectively. Title Pages will be prepared in manuscript.

Place	Date	Hour	Summary of Events and Information	Remarks and references to Appendices
TAILLY	9.1.16	8.30 am	2nd Lt. Troces - Orderly Officer. Demand from Colonnen for 304 rounds of 13 hr Shrapnel - lorry sent at once to bring on return from 1st Corps Railhead LAPUGNOY.	
		8.30 am	Lorry to LAPUGNOY supply for reserves for "dumnags" on which to chuck the ammunition.	
"	10.1.16	8.0 am	1st Lt. Rouck - Orderly Officer. Ten leaves out to R.E. for fatigue duty.	
		8.60 am	Further demand for 304 rounds of 13 hr Shrapnel lorry despatched. Arch & reported 1st Corps Railhead run out of 13 hr Shrapnel - N.C.O. i/c sent (N.6.B) to throw up there - lorry get back 9.50 hrs with ammunition.	Reference mark 36 A.S.coll 1/20500 DWK
			Lorry sent on to TREIZENNES	
"	11.1.16		Lt. Rubury - Orderly Officer.	
		8.0 am	10 lorries out on fatigue duty to R.E.	
		3.30 hrs	286 rounds Shrapnel sent to Colonnen. Lt Rubury to field cashier - draws pay - unable to get it.	SWB
"	12.1.16		Lt. Mali - Orderly Officer.	
		12.0 am	10 lorries out on fatigue work to R.E. B.D. Went three way from field cashier.	
		2.30 pm	456 rounds 13 hr Shrapnel to colonnen	WWM

WAR DIARY
or
INTELLIGENCE SUMMARY

(Erase heading not required.)

Army Form C. 2118

Place	Date	Hour	Summary of Events and Information	Remarks and references to Appendices
TAILLY	13.1.16	12.0 noon	2nd Lt Lucas - Orderly Officer. 16 Lorries out on R.E. fatigue work for the D.D. Count of enquiry held on the illegal absence of Pte Dunn of (7th 685 181). Paid out the men.	LTWR
"	14.1.16	8.0am	2nd Lt Roach - Orderly Officer. Two lorries to R.E. for fatigue work.	
		7.45am	Four lorries to CHARING CROSS ( ) BETHUNE Engineers 1st Corps.	
		11.0am	One lorry with 76 rounds 13/pr Shrapnel to Columns.	*Reference Map BETHUNE continued Scale 1/40,000
		11.30am	One lorry to cross roads L.11.A.10.3.* for fatigues.	
		12.30pm	One lorry at cross roads at ANNEQUIN F.30.A.2.8.* - Conveyance of Troops.	
		2.0pm	One lorry out with 500 bombs (Heavy Mk III).	LTWR
"	15.1.16	1.30	Lt Rubury - Orderly Officer. Ten lorries out on R.E. work for D.D.	LTWR
	16.1.16		Lt Nibbs - Orderly Officer.	
		11.30am	150. 2" T.M Bombs to 100 boxes of very light to columns	
		1.30pm	Nine lorries out on R.E. work for D.D.	LTWR

WAR DIARY
or
INTELLIGENCE SUMMARY

(Erase heading not required.)

Army Form C. 2118

Instructions regarding War Diaries and Intelligence Summaries are contained in F.S. Regs., Part II. and the Staff Manual respectively. Title Pages will be prepared in manuscript.

Place	Date	Hour	Summary of Events and Information	Remarks and references to Appendices
TA'LLY	17.1.16		2nd Lt Tween — Orderley Officer	
		11.30 am	540 rounds of 13 hr Shrapnel to Column	
		1.30	10 lorries out on fatigue work for R.E.	
		11.30	Long To VE R QVI GIVEVL for continuum estimes.	BZWK
"	18.1.16	10.30	2nd Lt Roach — Orderley Officer.	
			304 rounds of 13 hr Shrapnel to Column.	
			Brie Cm took up some spare gun parts to Column.	
			Lorry with 150 2" T.M bombs to Column.	
			Ten lorries out on R.E. fatigue work for D.D.	BZWK
TA'LLY	19.1.16	10.30	Lt Rubury — O. Officer.	
			228 rounds 13 Pr. Shrapnel & 5 boxes of Very's lights to Column.	
			Lt Lucas rushed O.C R.H.A. 2nd Lar Div.	
		1.30	10 lorries out on fatigue work for R.E. of 4o.D.	BZWK
"	20.1.16		Lt Nutal — Orderley Officer.	
		11.30	16 lorries on R.E. fatigue work.	
		12.30	600 very's lights (white) & 152 round 13 hr Shrapnel to Column.	BZWK

WAR DIARY
or
INTELLIGENCE SUMMARY
(Erase heading not required.)

Army Form C. 2118

Place	Date	Hour	Summary of Events and Information	Remarks and references to Appendices
TAILLY	21.1.16		2nd Lt Lucas. 1000 rounds S.A.A. 9480 rounds Webley Westminnes. 16 Lorries out on R.E fatigue work.	
"	22.1.16	11.30 am	2nd Lt Roser. 152 rounds of 13 pr Shrapnel — Column also 120 One inch & 720 1½" very's lights. 2 Lorries out to convey cook house stores from BETHUNE for the Dismounted Division. 1 Lorry to MERVILLE to convey stores to SAILLY LABOURSE.	WTWH WTWH
"	23.1.16 11.30		Lt Rubery – Orderly Officer. Ten Lorries to R.E. for fatigue work for the Dismounted Division. 364 rounds of 13 pr Shrapnel to Column returned at O.K. and returned.	WTWH
"	24.1.16 7.30 am		2nd Lt Nisbet – orderly Officer. 7 Lorries to convey men from BETHUNE to joint W. of VERMELLES for transport of troops.	
		2.30 pm	Lorry to Dismounted Division Ordinance Dump for stores.	BWH
"	25.1.16	10.0 am	2nd Lt Rowal – Orderly Officer. 304 rounds Shrapnel 13 pr Q F to Column	
		10.10	Lorry No 6552 DISEGERGUES to be telegrammed	
		12.0 noon	Six Lorries out on fatigue work for the R.E.	WTWH

WAR DIARY
INTELLIGENCE SUMMARY

Army Form C. 2118

Place	Date	Hour	Summary of Events and Information	Remarks and references to Appendices
TAILLY	26-1-16	10.30	2nd Lt. Roach. Orderly Officer. Lorry out for ordnance stores to VERAUQUEUIL.	
		11.30	Lorry out with 304 rounds 13 lb. Shrapnel to column refilled at OK railhead.	
		10.0 am	Two lorries with 608 rounds 13 lb. Shrapnel – refilled at OK and returned.	
		7.30	Orderly lorry out on fatigue duties transporting working party from trenches.	L/W.J.R.
	27-1-16		2nd Lt. Ruting Orderly Officer. 2nd Lt. Lucas goes on leave.	
		11.0 am	Three Lorries to transport Battalion from Tincles to Estrées.	
		2.30 am	Two lorries to bomb stores for T.M.	
		6.50 am	One lorry with 304 rounds of shrapnel to columns, refilled & returned to Park 10.40 am.	
		7.8 am	One lorry to 10' Coke dump for very's lights – Cartridges illuminating & 50mm 304 fuzes returned & columns & returned.	
		1.30 pm	Lorry to 10' corps dump for rifle grenades – these & returned empties. Arrived BOYCE unfilled took & found nothing generally satisfactory.	L/W.J.R.
	28-1-16		2nd Lt. Nisbet – Orderly Officer.	
		6.50 am	Lorry left with 304 rounds 13 in. Shrapnel & refilled at OK railhead & returned. (10.0 am)	
		7.45 am	" " " " " "	L/W.J.R.
	29-1-16	6.30 am	2nd Lt. Roach. Orderly Officer. Two lorries with 228 rounds of Shrapnel & 188 HE 4.5/20 fuzes also very light brackets etc.	
		6.0 am	Right lorries out for lorry one of both under Lt. Ruting. Lorries went to surprise at 10.30 am but did not receive the order till 10.45 am. Lorries came back having reach the Gate.	L/W.J.R.

Army Form C. 2118

WAR DIARY
or
INTELLIGENCE SUMMARY
(Erase heading not required.)

Instructions regarding War Diaries and Intelligence Summaries are contained in F. S. Regs., Part II. and the Staff Manual respectively. Title Pages will be prepared in manuscript.

Place	Date	Hour	Summary of Events and Information	Remarks and references to Appendices
TAILLY	30-1-16	11.30 am	Y- Return – Orderly Officer. Sick horses out on fatigue work for R.E. &c. No other horses out on ammunition work.	15W/h
"	31-1-16	8.30 / 11.30 am	Y- Visit – Orderly Officer. Lorry rolls thought lightly and three men to examine H.E. shell with M2 from VERMELLES fuzes. Sick horses out on fatigue work for conveyance of troops to & from VERMELLES.	15W/h
	1.2.16			

15W Howard
Captain 15C
Officer commanding the 2nd Cavalry Division Amm: Pk.

L of C

Confidential.

War Diary.

of

2nd Can. Div., Amm'n Park.

From 1st February to 29th February 1916

Vol XIV

Army Form C. 2118

WAR DIARY
or
INTELLIGENCE SUMMARY

(Erase heading not required.)

Instructions regarding War Diaries and Intelligence Summaries are contained in F. S. Regs., Part II. and the Staff Manual respectively. Title Pages will be prepared in manuscript.

Place	Date	Hour	Summary of Events and Information	Remarks and references to Appendices
TAILLY	1.2.16	2.30 pm	2nd Lt Rouse - Orderly Officer. 8 Lorries to convey troops from BETHUNE to VERMELLES.	WJWJ
		6.40 pm	Lorry out to Bomb stores for grenades etc. then to columns and return. (11.15am)	
"	2.2.16	11.0 am	Lt Railway Orderly Officer. Three lorries out for stores.	
		2.30 pm	Returning from O.C. 1st C.A.P. to change remaining H.E. shell with 80 fuzes for 85 fuzes over gains No 1. Lorry leaves left for O.x railhead with above to railhead with 1380 rounds H.E. 80 fuze over gain- gain No 1. (7.45 am).	WJWJ
"	3.2.16	12.9 midday	Lt Nisbet - Orderly Officer. Six lorries out on R.E. fatigue work to VERMELLES.	
		2.30 pm	Brought for 304 rounds of ammunition lorry away 2.35 D column relieves park at reloading at O.x railhead at 5.20 am	
		2.15 pm	Lorry out to Corps Dump for T.M. ammunition Marco to columns & return.	WJWJ
"	4.2.15	6.30 am	2nd Lt Roach Orderly Officer Snow Lorries out to convey working party. Lorry with 304 rounds of ammunition from BETHUNE to VERMELLES & columns	
		6.30 pm		5.0 am
"	5.2.15		Lt Railway went on Leave - Lt Nisbet Orderly Officer. Six Lorries out on R.E. Fatigue work to VERMELLES	WJWJ
		7.0 am	Lorry out to collect 40rys-light from Corps Park dump thence to columns & return.	WJWJ

Army Form C. 2118

WAR DIARY
or
INTELLIGENCE SUMMARY
(Erase heading not required.)

Instructions regarding War Diaries and Intelligence Summaries are contained in F. S. Regs., Part II. and the Staff Manual respectively. Title Pages will be prepared in manuscript.

Place	Date	Hour	Summary of Events and Information	Remarks and references to Appendices
TAILLY	6.2.16	7.0	2nd Lt. Lucas – Orderly Officer.	
			Seven lorries out on R.E fatigue work to VERMELLES.	
		11.30	One lorry to columns with 284 rounds of 13 pr Q.F. Shrapnel.	
"	7.2.16	6.30	2nd Lt. Roach – Orderly Officer.	
			Seven lorries out for conveyance of troops from BETHUNE to VERMELLES.	
		7.0	304 rounds of 13 pr Q.F Shrapnel to Columns. Lorries to Railhead to refill and return.	
		10.0	Lorry to VERQUIGNEUL for Ordnance stores.	
		2.10 pm	Paid out the men.	
"	8.2.16	7.10	Lt. Mahil - Orderly Officer.	
			304 rounds of 13 pr Q.F Shrapnel to columns thence to Railhead to refill and return.	
		1.0	Ten lorries out for conveyance of troops from BETHUVE to VERMELLES.	
"	9.2.16	6.00	2nd Lt Facey – Orderly Officer.	
			Seven lorries out to Railway troops from BETHUNE to Vermelles.	
		9.0	One lorry with 304 rounds Shrapnel to Columns thence to OK. road head to return.	
		2.0	Eight lorries out for conveyance of troops from VERMELLES to BETHUNE.	
"	10.2.16	9.0 am	2nd Lt. Rouse – Orderly Officer.	
			200 rounds 13 pr Q.F Shrapnel to columns hence to Ox-railhead to refill & return.	
		10.30 am	Eight lorries for conveyance of troops of the dismounted Division from BETHUNE to VERMELLES.	
		11.30	Six lorries out on R.E E.B fatigue work.	
"	11.2.16		Lt. Mahil – Orderly Officer.	
			2 How with Battery No 5 from Brent move thence to Philosophe.	
			3 lorries to PHILOSOPHE conveying troops BETHUVE.	

WAR DIARY
or
INTELLIGENCE SUMMARY

(Erase heading not required.)

Army Form C. 2118

Place	Date	Hour	Summary of Events and Information	Remarks and references to Appendices
TAILLY	12.2.16		2nd Lt Irving – Orderly Officer. One lorry to Railhead with 306 rounds Q.F. 13 pr. Shrapnel. Refilled at Ox Railhead & returned to Park. Six lorries out on R.E. fatigue work. Two lorries to Auchel for baths for men. Two lorries to Philosophe on fatigue work. Company played 4/5th Divisional Supply Column – & drew 1–1.	WJWR
"	13.2.16		2nd Lt Roach – Orderly Officer. Two lorries out to PHILOSOPHE on fatigue work. 228 rounds 13 pr Q.F. & 70 columns. Refill of Ox railhead & return to Park. Two lorries with 76 4" T.M. Ammunition and 1050 1" very lights	WJWR
"	15.2.16	6.0 a.m. 8.0 a.m. 9.0 p.m. 1.30 p.m. " 2.0 pm	Orderly Officer – Lieutenant Niabet. 3 lorries out to PHILOSOPHE Cross roads on R.E. fatigue work. 5 " " NOVELLES on R.E. fatigue work. Two lorries out- with 456 rounds 13 pr Q.F. Shrapnel. refilled at Ox Railhead & returned. Lorry to CHOQUES for coal goal. 3 lorries to columns with 760 rounds 13 pr Q.F. Shrapnel. refilled at Ox Railhead & returned. 1 " " " with bombs – (Mills) 1 lorry to AUCHEL for men for baths.	WJWR
"	16.2.15	10.30	Orderly Officer Lieutenant Roach. Captain Howard goes on leave. Lt Rubury returns off leave. Lorry to Columns with Newton Rifle Grenades 96 rounds & T.M. Ammunition 4" 100 rounds	WJWR
"	16.2.16	2.15 pm	Orderly Officer – Lieut Holgreaves. Lorry to Columns with 300 rounds T.M. Ammunition 4".	WJWR

WAR DIARY
or
INTELLIGENCE SUMMARY

(Erase heading not required.)

Army Form C. 2118

Place	Date	Hour	Summary of Events and Information	Remarks and references to Appendices
TAILLY	17.2.16		Orderly Officer 2/Lt Rowan	
		6.30am	Two lorries out on R.E. fatigue work.	
		7.0am	One lorry to H.Q. of 7th R.I.F. HESDIGNEUL.	
		8.30am	Lorry out to IV Army Mun. Reserve School BETHUNE.	
		9.0am	" " to CRE 16th Div. at AMETTES.	
		10.30	Two lorries to columns with Newton Rifle grenades 144 rounds.	
		2.0	Lorry to CHOQUES for wood.	WJWR
"	18.2.16		Orderly Officer 2/Lt Lucas	
		7.0am	4 Lorries to H.Q. 17th R.I.F. HESDIGNEUL for fatigue work.	
		"	3 " " 6th " " " "	
		"	1 lorry for conveyance of Blanket etc.	
		"	" to CRE 16th division to convoir at Annette.	
		10.30	Lorry to Reserve School to draw 150 Rifle grenades thence to columns to deliver the same.	
		2.0	Delivered 232 rounds of 13 in O.F. shrapnel & 1 column & refilled equipment to Parcs. A.D.O.S. L. 75/1.20 ADS 2 mj 5 884/15	
		4	Railway wagons orders to report at H. Won Office. A.D.O 52 I/5/1.20 A 192 in j	
		4	Railway visit A A 2 m j with reference in to the above orders.	WJWR
"	19.2.16		Orderly Officer 2/Lt Nisbet.	
		7.30am	4 Lorries to ESTRES BLANCHE H.Q. of 11th Hants. to take Baggage, stores etc. to EQUIN. LES. MINES	
		7.0am	1 lorry to AMETTES to CRE 16th Division.	
		6.30am	Two lorries on R.E. fatigue work.	
			All necessary weekly return sent in to 10th Corps A.P. and A A 2 in g 7 nd Corps Div.	WJWR

Army Form C. 2118

WAR DIARY
or
INTELLIGENCE SUMMARY
(Erase heading not required.)

Instructions regarding War Diaries and Intelligence Summaries are contained in F.S. Regs., Part II. and the Staff Manual respectively. Title Pages will be prepared in manuscript.

Place	Date	Hour	Summary of Events and Information	Remarks and references to Appendices
TAILLY	20.2.16		Orderly Officer 2nd Lt Fraser.	
		10.30	Lorry with - T.M. Light - 1½" rds 50 TM Heavy 1½" rds 50 - TM 2" (Smoke) Rds 100. Nose-cap - No 110 &... from G.H.Q. As replace 3070 to be returned to D.D.T Southdown. Lt Redway left for Perth for England to report to War Office.	WD/W
"	21.2.16		Orderly Officer - 2nd Lt Rouch. Drew 1800 Mills No 5 to complete establishment	
		2.20 pm	Issued 228 Rounds Shrapnel 13 Pr & rifles at Ox railhead. Received application Drawn tomorrow - sent in Marchings-out details to A.C. 1st Corps Parks.	WD/W
AVROULT	22.2.16	9.45 am	Orderly Officer 2nd Lt Lucas. Park off TAILLY 8.45 a.m and arrived at AVROULT at 12 o noon after a successful run. Captain Stephenson returned off Leave. Park issued 106,000 rounds S.A.A. 4 & 5th January.	WD/W
"	23.2.16		Orderly Officer - 2nd Lt Roach. Supplied Columns with 296,000 rds SAA. Drew money from Field Cashier & paid out men.	WD/W
"	24.2.16	9.0 am	Orderly Officer 2nd Lt Lucas. 3 lorries with 1000 rounds of Shrapnel to 5 Horsed. 2nd Lt Wight arrived Depoted for duty Vice Lt Redway	WD/W
"	25.2.16	10.30	Orderly Officer - 2nd Lt Wight. 7 horses & Boulogne tender 2nd Lt Wight - They drew 3000000 rounds S.A.A. 1572 Mills No 5 grenades and 31 boxes of Webby pistol - got arrived up & routes not return next night. One lorry returned at about 4.30 having carts-.	WD/W
"	26.2.16	1.30 pm	Orderly Officer 2nd Lt Rouch. 604 rounds of 13 pr A.F Shrapnel 8,132 from the trucks taken in 3 lorries to Railhead at ARQUES 3 Lorries each at 60 from BOULOG N.E and 3 each arrived 11.0 hrs.	WD/W

1875 Wt. W593/826 1,000,000 4/15 J.B.C.&A. A.D.S.S./Forms/C. 2118.

WAR DIARY
or
INTELLIGENCE SUMMARY

(Erase heading not required.)

Army Form C. 2118

Place	Date	Hour	Summary of Events and Information	Remarks and references to Appendices
AV ROVLT	27.2.16		Orderly Officer 2nd Lieut Lucas. All roads closed to Motor Lorries on account of Snow & Thaw - Nothing to Report.	WSWTk
"	28.2.16		Orderly Officer 2nd Lieut Lucas. All roads close to Motor Lorries on account of Snow & Thaw. Nothing to Report.	WSWTk
"	29.2.16		Orderly Officer 2nd Lieut Wight. All roads closed as on 28th to 27th - Nothing to report.	WSWTk

March 1st 1916

BWHowsons
Captain RGC
O.C. 2nd Cavalry Division Ammunition Park

Confidential.

War Diary.
of.
2nd Cav. Div. Ammn Pk.

From 1st February to 29th February 1916.

L of C.

CONFIDENTIAL

WAR DIARY
of
2nd Cavalry Division Ammn Park

From 1st to 31st March 1916.

Vol XVIII

Army Form C. 2118

WAR DIARY
or
INTELLIGENCE SUMMARY
(Erase heading not required.)

Instructions regarding War Diaries and Intelligence Summaries are contained in F.S. Regs., Part II. and the Staff Manual respectively. Title Pages will be prepared in manuscript.

Place	Date	Hour	Summary of Events and Information	Remarks and references to Appendices
AVROULT	1.3.16		2nd Lt Roach - Orderly Officer. All rounds still closed to M.T. 200 H sent down transport for 81,000 rds of S.A.A.	
"	2.3.16	9.0am	2nd Lt Wight - Orderly Officer. Lorry to Coloume with 80,000 rounds of S.A.A. also 3 4½ Howitzer & 9,000 S.A.A. to 3rd Divisions	
"	3.3.16	8.0am	2nd Lt Roach - Orderly Officer. 2nd Lt Lucas to BOULOGNE with eight lorries to collect S.A.A. grenades, very Lights etc - Two of them lorries broke down and sent for others to bring them in - all lorries back by 10.30 hrs. Lt Naslet returned off leave.	
"	4.3.16	8.0am	Lt Naslet - Orderly Officer. One lorry to Coloume with S.A.A. - One lorry to 5th Brigade & one to 3rd & 4½ with S.A.A. grenades & very Lights	
"	5.3.16		2nd Lt Wight - Orderly Officer. No lorries out - Nothing to report	
"	6.3.16	8.0am	2nd Lt Roach - Orderly Officer. Lorry to Various regiments with S.A.A. grenades etc.	
"	7.3.16		2nd Lt Roach - Orderly Officer - No lorries out & nothing to report.	
"	8.3.16		2nd Lt Facus - Orderly Officer - No lorries out & Nothing to report.	
"	9.3.16	7.30am	2nd Lt Naslet - Orderly Officer. Lorry with wheels to HAZEBROUCK.	
"	10.3.16		2nd Lt Wight - No lorries out & nothing to report. Lorry to Coloume for relief - going to Coloume for column of S.A.A.	
"	11.3.16	9.0am	2nd Lieut Roach - Orderly Officer. Car to Ammunition Colonne with spare gun parts. Thence to A.O.H. & 60 D. Bn with rifle ammunition	

WAR DIARY or INTELLIGENCE SUMMARY

Army Form C. 2118

(Erase heading not required.)

Place	Date	Hour	Summary of Events and Information	Remarks and references to Appendices
AVROULT	12.3.16		2nd Lt Lucas - Orderly Officer - Nothing to report & No lorries out	
"	13.3.16		Lt Nisbet - Orderly Officer	
		7.30pm	Vauxhall car to OY Railhead for rifle grenades - lorry also out for coal & wood	
"	14.3.16		Lt Wight - Orderly Officer	
			Confirming short Rebel - A very successful meeting	
"	15.3.16	8.0 am	2nd Lt Roach - Orderly Officer	
			Lorry out to 3rd LLa & 5th Brigade with R.G. Grenades & Mills No 5	
"	16.3.16		2nd Lt Lucas - Orderly Officer - No lorries out - Nothing to report	
"	17.3.16		Lt Nisbet - Orderly Officer	
		7.30 am	Four lorries to BOUVIGNE truck & 2nd Lt Roach - 2nd Lt Lucas RFA drew SAA	
"	18.3.16	9.10 am	Lt Wight - Orderly Officer	
			Lorry to Colonne with SAA	
"	19.3.16		2nd Lt Roach - Orderly Officer - No lorries out and willing to report	
"	20.3.16		2nd Lt Lucas - Orderly Officer	
		7.30 am	Sunbeam Car - one lorry to OY Railhead to collect grenades for Machine Gunners	
"	21.3.16		Lt Nisbet - Orderly Officer	
			Lorry to 3rd L & 5th Brigade & with 300 Mls 2 & 40 R/G grenades for being shipped to cars	
"	22.3.16	10.30	2nd Lt Wight - orderly Officer	
			Lorry & 6 men to O.C.A.S.C. for fatigue work	
"	23.3.16		2nd Lt Lucas - Orderly Officer	
			2nd Lt Roach went on leave.	
"	24.3.16	7.30 am	Lt Nisbet - orderly Officer	
			Lorry and 6 men as fatigue party for cutting wood	

Army Form C. 2118

WAR DIARY
or
INTELLIGENCE SUMMARY
(Erase heading not required.)

Instructions regarding War Diaries and Intelligence Summaries are contained in F. S. Regs., Part II. and the Staff Manual respectively. Title Pages will be prepared in manuscript.

Place	Date	Hour	Summary of Events and Information	Remarks and references to Appendices
AVROULT	25.3.16	7.30 am	2nd Lieut. Wight - Orderly Officer. Lorry to R.E. for fatigue work. Lorry to O.C.A.S.C. for fatigue work cutting wood	WZW/O
"	26.3.16	7.30 am	2nd Lt. Lucas - Orderly Officer. Lorry to Cy railhead for practice bombs.	WZW/O
"	27.3.16	7.30 am	Lt. Nutt - Orderly Officer. Lorry out for wood cutting O.C.A.O.C. fatigue work.	WZW/O
"	28.3.16	7.30 am	2nd Lt. Wight - Orderly Officer. Lorry out to 3rd Line & 5th Bgde to issue Mills & Rifle grenades for practice purposes.	WZW/O
"	29.3.16	8.45 am	2nd Lt. Lucas - Orderly Officer. O.C. visits O.C. No 9 Armoured car-section & notes reference to refilling of the vehicles being stores in the park at/near WZW/O	WZW/O
"	30.3.16		Lt. Nutt - Orderly Officer - Nothing to report.	WZW/O
"	31.3.16		2nd Lt. Wight - Orderly Officer. Lorry to O.C.A.S.C. for fatigue work - Sent in monthly returns.	WZW/O

April 1st 1916

W.W. Howard
Capt A.S.C.
O.C. 2nd Cavalry Division Ammunition Park

L of C.

Confidential

War Diary

of

2nd Cavalry Division Ammn Park

from 1st to 30th April 1916

Vol XIX

WAR DIARY
or
INTELLIGENCE SUMMARY

(Erase heading not required.)

Army Form C. 2118

Place	Date	Hour	Summary of Events and Information	Remarks and references to Appendices
AVROULT	1.4.16	7.30 am	2nd Lt Roach – Orderly Officer. Lorry out for R E to ABEELE and return.	
"	2.4.16		2nd Lt Lucas – Orderly Officer. 2nd Lt Gallacher arrived on the park to take over from 2nd Lt Lucas as R F A officer attached.	
"	3.4.16	7.30 8.0	Lt Nudd – Orderly Officer. Lorry to R E for fatigue work. Lorry to O.C.A.S.C. for fatigue work. 2nd Lt Lucas goes on leave prior to transfer to Ammunition Column	
"	4.4.16	7.30 am	2nd Lt Wyld – Orderly Officer. Lorry to R E for fatigue work. Two lorries to O of ordnance for grenades – S A A Lorry to St OMER for workshop material	
"	5.4.16	8.45 am	2nd Lt Roach – Orderly Officer. Lorry with 3 others to railhead and on with 51st ammunition to O.W railhead. All shrapnel. To O.V Railhead Both lorries then to D Battery to column with empty lorries – Gone round one full in brigade.	
"	6.4.16	6.30 am	2nd Lt Gallacher – Orderly Officer. Lorries picked up ammunition from D battery & column. There two lorries to O Y and two to O.W. The two lorries from O.V. proceeded to O.W. and then all four returned with empty lorries.	
"	7.4.16	6.0 am 6.0 am 6.30 am 10.30 am	Lt Nudd – Orderly Officer. Two lorries to J battery with empties, loaded with 600 rounds shrapnel 13 pr. A.F. fuses cloned to O.Y. Two lorries to E battery with empties, loaded with 600 rounds shrapnel 13 pr. A.F. and return to park. One lorry to column with empties, loaded on remaining rounds shrapnel 13 pr. A.F. in it return to park. Ammunition collected from E battery & column and in 3 lorries to O.W & one to O.Y. All shrapnel 13 pr now withdrawn	

Army Form C. 2118

WAR DIARY
or
INTELLIGENCE SUMMARY

(Erase heading not required.)

Instructions regarding War Diaries and Intelligence Summaries are contained in F.S. Regs., Part II. and the Staff Manual respectively. Title Pages will be prepared in manuscript.

Place	Date	Hour	Summary of Events and Information	Remarks and references to Appendices
AVROULT	8.4.16	7.0 am	2nd Lt. Roach - Orderly Officer. Lorry to O.C. A.S.C. for fatigue work.	
"	9.4.16		2nd Lt. Wight - Orderly Officer - Nothing to report.	15/4/16
"	10.4.16	7.30 am 9.0 am	2nd Lt. Gallaher - Orderly Officer. Lorry to R.E. for fatigue work. Lorry to OY for ground ules it for practice purposes for the cavalry Regiments.	15/4/16
"	11.4.16		Lt. Nisbet - Orderly Officer. Lorry out DADOS of Brigades to deliver grenades.	15/4/16
"	12.4.16	1.0 hour	Lt. Wight - Orderly Officer. Lorry to S. Column for Lorries Brigades. Lt. Gallaher - Orderly officer willing goes on leave. 2nd Lt. Jones returning to go to Colmars	15/4/16
"	13.4.16	7.30 am	2nd Lt. Roach - Orderly Officer. Lorry to O.C. A.S.C. on fatigue work & curteri B.R.E. for down purpose.	15/4/16
"	14.4.16		Lt. Nisbet - Orderly Officer - Nothing to report.	15/4/16
"	15.4.16	7.30 am	2nd Lt. Wight - Orderly Officer. Lorry to R.E. for fatigue work.	15/4/16
"	16.4.16		2nd Lt. Roach - Orderly Officer - Nothing to report -	15/4/16
"	17.4.16	8.0 am 7.0 am	Lt. Nisbet - Orderly Officer. Lorry to OY railhead for practice grenades. Lorry to O.C. A.S.C. on fatigue work.	20/4/16
"	18.4.16	9.0 am 10.0 am 6.0 am	2nd Lt. Wight - Orderly Officer. Lorry out to 3rd L.H. & 5th L.H. Brigades to deliver grenades etc for practice purposes. Two lorries to O.C. A.S.C. for fatigue work. Lorry & Limber for wheels for M.G. Coy.	15/4/16

WAR DIARY / INTELLIGENCE SUMMARY

Army Form C. 2118

Place	Date	Hour	Summary of Events and Information	Remarks and references to Appendices
AVROULT	19.4.16		2nd Lt Roach – Orderly Officer – Nothing to report.	
"	20.4.16	7.30 am	Lt Nisbet – Orderly Officer.	
		9.0 am	Lorries to RE and OC ASC on fatigue work. H.E.	
			Three lorries to Coternen with 712 rounds 13 pr A.F. and 85 fuzes returned with 900 rounds H.E. 4½ fuze.	
		2.0 pm	Two lorries to D Battery & two to each with 264 13 pr A.F. H.E. with 85 fuzes. The four lorries returned with 456 rounds from each battery. (H.E. 4½/20 fuzes).	Initials
"	21.4.16		2nd Lt Wight – Orderly Officer	
		6.0 am	Lorry out early to OY with 300 rounds of 4½/20 fuzed H.E. with unfuzed 4½	
		8.0 am	Six lorries with H.E. (4½ go fuze) to be returned to OY (Total returned to OY 1850 rounds this day.) three lorries	
		10.30 am	Brought back 49 rounds of 85 fuzes and 820 rounds of 13 pr fuzes no 2 gain (all H.E.) Total 868 rounds	
			Three empty lorries to Coternen to bring back 755 rounds of H.E. 13 pr A.F. 4½/20 fuzes	
		2.0 pm	Two lorries with 264 H.E. rounds of 85 fuzes to E Battery and return with 456 rounds 4½/20 fuzes	Initials
"	22.4.16		2nd Lt Roach – Orderly Officer	
		9.0 am	From lorries to OY railhead with 1215 rounds of H.E. 4½/20 fuze and returned with empty ammunition for practice on 16 rounds	
			85 fuzes required to complete C. in lieu thereof of 900 rounds of H.E. were completed on port. 12 rounds 4½/20 still to go to OY	Initials
"	23.4.16		2nd Lt Yatterlee – Orderly Officer – Nothing to report.	
"	24.4.16	7.30 am	Lt Nisbet – Orderly Officer	
		9.0 am	Lorry to RE on fatigue work	
			Lorry lorry to OY for grenades Bombs etc – Returned 12 rounds 4½/20 fuze machines on 22.4.16	Initials
"	25.4.16	9.30 am	3rd Lt Wight – Orderly Officer	
			Lorry to OY for ammunition Bombs etc from the RE	
		9.15 am	Lorry out to Wass grenades for practice to Brigade H.Q.	Initials
"	26.4.16	7.30 am	2nd Lt Roach – Orderly Officer	
			Lorry out for personnel signals tools bombs and grenades to RE on the way letter	
			Lorry to RC ASC for fatigue work	Initials

WAR DIARY
or
INTELLIGENCE SUMMARY

(Erase heading not required.)

Army Form C. 2118

Place	Date	Hour	Summary of Events and Information	Remarks and references to Appendices
AVROULT	27.4.16	7.30	2nd Lieutenant Hollicum - Orderly Officer. Two lorries out and one to O.C.A.S.C. for fatigue work.	157/104
"	28.4.16	7.30	Lt. Nisbet - Orderly Officer. Lorry to R.E. on fatigue work.	159/114
"	29.4.16	7.30	2nd Lt. Wright - Orderly Officer. Lorry to 2nd F.S. R.E. for fatigue work.	157/104
"	30.4.16		2nd Lt. Roach - Orderly Officer. Nothing to report.	179/11A

May 1st 1916

W.W. Howard Capt ASC
O.C. 2nd Cavalry Division Ammunition Park.

Confidential

War Diary
of
2nd Cavalry Division Amm'n Park

From 1st March to 31st March 1916

Confidential

War Diary

of

2nd Cavalry Division Ammn Park.

From 1st to 30th April 1916

Confidential
War Diary
of
2nd Cavalry Division, Ammn Sub Park

From 1st May 1916   To   31st May 1916

WAR DIARY
~~INTELLIGENCE SUMMARY~~
(Erase heading not required.)

Army Form C. 2118

Instructions regarding War Diaries and Intelligence Summaries are contained in F. S. Regs., Part II. and the Staff Manual respectively. Title Pages will be prepared in manuscript.

Place	Date	Hour	Summary of Events and Information	Remarks and references to Appendices
AVROULT	1.5.16	7.0 am	2nd Lt Gallacher – Orderly Officer. Two lorries out on R.E. fatigue work. Lorry out to O.C.A.S.C. for supply work.	
		8.0 am	Lorry out to collect Practice Grenade from O.Y.	
		2.0 pm	Lorry out for Workshop material.	DWH
"	2.5.16	6.30 am	2nd Lt Pelt – Orderly Officer. Two lorries to J Brigade H.Q. – one to I Battery and one to 1/16 Bgde to assist in change of billets.	
		9.0 am	Lorry out to issue Practice Grenades to Brigades H.Q. *Note Lorries lent to 5th Brigade for two days.	DWH
"	3.5.16	6.0 am	2nd Lt Wright – Orderly Officer. Lorry out to O.Y. for 24 rds: 13 hr R.F. Shrapnel – Three to each Battery to deliver 3 for practice purposes	DWH
		6.30 am	Lorry out to O.C.A.S.C. for supply work.	
"	4.5.16	7.10 am	2nd Lt Roach – Orderly Officer. Three lorries sent on R.E. fatigue work. 12,000 rounds to 3 M.G. Squadron.	DWH
"	5.5.16	7.0 am	2nd Lt Gallacher – Orderly Officer. Five lorries out on R.E. fatigue work. One lorry lent to Divisional Supplies for two days & one to H.Q. for one day.	DWH
"	6.5.16	7.0 am	2nd Lt Naish – Orderly Officer. Lorry to R.E. on fatigue work.	DWH
"	7.5.16		2nd Lt Wright – Orderly Officer. Lorry D.R.E. on fatigue work – also one to A.S.C. for supply work.	DWH
"	8.5.16	7.0 am	2nd Lt Roach – Orderly Officer. 3 Lorries out on R.E. fatigue work.	
		8.30 am	Lorry to S. charged for Practice grenades.	DWH
"	9.5.16		2nd Lt Gallacher – Orderly Officer. Lorry out issuing grenades to Brigades H.Q. Two lorries out on R.E. fatigue.	DWH
"	10.5.16		Lt Wright – Orderly Officer. Two lorries out on R.E. fatigue work. 276 rounds to Workshop for Guns and 2000 rounds S.M.A. ammunition –	DWH

Army Form C. 2118

WAR DIARY
or
~~INTELLIGENCE SUMMARY~~
(Erase heading not required.)

Instructions regarding War Diaries and Intelligence Summaries are contained in F. S. Regs., Part II. and the Staff Manual respectively. Title Pages will be prepared in manuscript.

Place	Date	Hour	Summary of Events and Information	Remarks and references to Appendices
AVROULT	11.5.16		2nd Lt. Wright - Orderly Officer	
		7.0 am	Major Stewart goes on leave. Two lorries out on R.E. fatigue work.	
"	12.5.16	7.0 am	2nd Lt. Rosser - Orderly Officer. Three lorries out on R.E. fatigue work.	W.W.R
"	13.5.16	7.0 am	2nd Lt. Gallacher - Orderly Officer. Two lorries out on R.E. fatigue work.	W.W.R
"	14.5.16	—	2nd Lt. Wright - Orderly Officer - Nothing to report.	W.W.R
"	15.5.16	7.0 am	2nd Lt. Rosser - Orderly Officer. Two lorries out on R.E. fatigue work.	W.W.R
"	16.5.16	7.0 am	2nd Lt. Gallacher - Orderly Officer. One lorry to Boulogne Ft. 9+9 and one to R.E.	W.W.R
"	17.5.16	7.0 am	2nd Lt. Wright - Orderly Officer. One lorry to O.Y. railhead for supply work - could not be utilised for practice gas munition. 2nd Lt Gallacher & applies - one lorry on fatigue work.	W.W.R
"	18.5.16	7.0 am 9.30 am	2nd Lt. Rosser - Orderly Officer. Two lorries and 20 O.F.S.C. for supplies work sent one to R.E. on fatigue work. Lorry out to 3rd & 10 & 6th Brigade Hqrs & 171 to deliver grenades, ammunition, etc.	W.W.R
"	19.5.16	7.0 am	2nd Lt. Gallacher - Orderly Officer. Lorry out on R.E. fatigue work. Major Stewart returns off leave.	W.W.R
"	20.5.16	7.0 am	2nd Lt. Nisbet - Orderly Officer. Lorry out on R.E. fatigue work.	W.W.R
"	21.5.16		2nd Lt. Wright - Orderly Officer - Nothing to report.	W.W.R
"	22.5.16		2nd Lt. Rosser - Orderly Officer. Lorry out on R.E. fatigue work.	W.W.R
"	23.5.16	7.0 am 7.30 am	2nd Lt. Gallacher - Orderly Officer. Two lorries out on R.E. fatigue work. One lorry out to camp common and Lt. Nisbet goes on leave.	W.W.R
"	24.5.16		2nd Lt. Wright - Orderly Officer. Lorry out 2nd Lt. Gallacher (Gunner Officer) to draw grenades for forward trenches for the garrison. One lorry out on R.E. fatigue work.	W.W.R

1875 Wt. W593/826 1,000,000 4/15 J.B.C. & A. A.D.S.S./Forms/C. 2118.

WAR DIARY

INTELLIGENCE SUMMARY

(Erase heading not required.)

Army Form C. 2118

Place	Date	Hour	Summary of Events and Information	Remarks and references to Appendices
AVROULT	25.5.16	7.0 am	Lt Roach - Orderly Officer. Three lorries out on R.E. fatigue work. Received notification that one officer & fifty men are to go chopping branches at Blendecques.	125/K
"	26.5.16	7.0 am	2nd Lt Gallacher - Orderly Officer. One lorry out on R.E. fatigue work.	126/K
"	27.5.16	11.30 am 9.0 am	Lt Wight - Orderly Officer. Three lorries for conveying cinder & tools to horse lines. One lorry for conveyance of hurt chaser.	125/K 127/K
"	28.5.16		Lt Roach - Orderly Officer. Nothing to report.	128/K
"	29.5.16	7.0 am	2nd Lt Gallacher - Orderly Officer. Lorry out on R.E. fatigue work. Lt Roach out & 50 men to go to point H 14 d (Sheet 28) to dig trenches similar to all actions previous.	129/K 127/K
"	30.5.16		Lt Wight - Orderly Officer. - Nothing to report.	
"	31.5.16		2nd Lt Gallacher - Orderly Officer. Lorry to O.Y. Railhead with 2nd Lt Gallacher to collect smoke grenades for Division H.Q.	

In the Field
June 1st 1916

L.W. Howorth
Major A.S.C.
O.C. 2nd Cavalry Division Ammunition Park.

Confidential

War Diary

2nd Cavalry Divisional Army Troops

From 1st May 1916   to   31st May 1916.

Army Form C. 2118

WAR DIARY
or
INTELLIGENCE SUMMARY
(Erase heading not required.)

Instructions regarding War Diaries and Intelligence Summaries are contained in F.S. Regs., Part II. and the Staff Manual respectively. Title Pages will be prepared in manuscript.

Place	Date	Hour	Summary of Events and Information	Remarks and references to Appendices
AVROULT	13.6.16	-	Lt Gallaher - Orderly Officer - Nothing to report	
"	14.6.16	8.0 am	Lt Mistol - Orderly Officer. 19 Zomm men. Lt Wight accompanied by Lt Gallaher proceeded to O.W. Pepling with 13 hr AFS lorries and returned to EBBLINGHAM and supplied A and C with 10 to 80 rounds and E and J Batteries with 792 each. 3 Lorries remained at EBBLINGHAM contain 5 new gun parts and 1500 rounds per B.E. gun. The remainder returned to park.	L.W.
"	15.6.16	-	Detachment at EBBLINGHAM proceeded to STEENVOORDE via the Wight attached to Canadian A.S.P.	
"	16.6.16	-	Four lorries to RC2 with empty cartridge ammunition (13 pr.) boxes	
"	17.6.16	-	Nothing to report.	
"	18.6.16	7.30 am	Lorry to R.E.	
"	19.6.16	4.30 pm	Receiving orders to be moving Zomm out. 50 returned surplus ammunition. Lorries returning. Two lorry lorries of surplus ammunition from 2nd and 3rd Bdes returned 8 of 2nd.	
"	20.6.16		Lt Rea - Orderly Officer. Orders to move for front - Zomm to 5D Park 8 am. 6 carried surplus ammunition	
HAZEBROUCK	21.6.16	8.30 am	Lt Mistol - Orderly Officer. Whole park move to war billets (this detachment of 4 lorries under 2/Lt Wight) at RV2 Post Guard N of HAZEBROUCK arrived at 11.30 after a successful journey.	
"	22.6.16	6.30 am	Lt Roach - Orderly Officer. One lorry for Div HQ at 10.10 am and two lorries to Divisional Regt & Liam used as motor Detachment performed parts leaving slowdown worth.	
"	23.6.16	7.30 am	Lt Gallaher - Orderly Officer Lorry to LUMBRES & WAVRANS & LUA U4 surplus & lorry ammunition etc.	
"	24.6.16	10.30	Lt Mistol - Orderly Officer One lorry to OV LUBB surplus ammunition & down to RC2 with surplus ammunition & tons for RE.	

WAR DIARY
INTELLIGENCE SUMMARY
(Erase heading not required.)

Army Form C. 2118

Instructions regarding War Diaries and Intelligence Summaries are contained in F.S. Regs., Part II. and the Staff Manual respectively. Title Pages will be prepared in manuscript.

Place	Date	Hour	Summary of Events and Information	Remarks and references to Appendices
HAZEBROUCK	25.6.16	10.30 am	2/Lt Wight - Orderly Officer. One lorry out - Billeliers. 1600 rounds to Column which is now up to establishment. Lorries refilled at Dy.	Intel
"	26.6.16	2.0 pm	2/Lt Roach - Orderly Officer. Lorry to Dy with 23,000 round surplus S.A.A. from II Division.	Intel
"	27.6.16	2.30 pm	2/Lt Ballanlure - Orderly Officer. Lorry to Column with 30mm A.A. gun parts, S.A.A. etc.	Intel
"	29.6.16	11.30 am	2/Lt Wight - Orderly Officer. 2/Lt Wight and 50 men detached on fatigue work - making a railway. Two lorries to convey these men to LA CRÈCHE 1/2 mile S.E. of BAILLEUL.	
		11.0 am	One lorry to 2nd Cavalry Field Ambulance at Oxy and to the 5th Cavalry Field Ambulance in its convoy went for a Ammn. before to LA CRÈCHE.	Intel
"	29.6.16	2.45 pm	2nd/Lt Gyllen...- Orderly Officer. Lorry with S.A.A. to A.O.O.14.	Intel
"	30.6.16	8.0 am	2/Lt Roach - Orderly Officer. Lorry out on fatigue work to the Division Front at LUM BRES.	Intel

July 1st 1916.

WWHoward
Major A.S.C.
O.C. 2nd Cavalry Division Ammunition Park.

2c

L.B.C. Bx21

Confidential

War Diary
of

2nd Can. Div. Ammn. Park

From 1st June 30th June 1916

CONFIDENTIAL.

WAR DIARY

of

2nd Cavalry Divisional Ammunition Park.

From: 1st July to 31st July. 1916.

(Volume XXIII).

WAR DIARY

Army Form C. 2118

Instructions regarding War Diaries and Intelligence Summaries are contained in F.S. Regs., Part II. and the Staff Manual respectively. Title Pages will be prepared in manuscript.

INTELLIGENCE SUMMARY

(Erase heading not required.)

Place	Date	Hour	Summary of Events and Information	Remarks and references to Appendices
HAZEBROUCK	July 1st, 2nd and 3rd		Nothing to report.	WEWR
"	4.7.16	10.0 am	Lorry to ambulance stores at CASSEL for oil blankets for dressing party – Three with them & supplies of dressings	WEWR
"	July 5 & 6		Nothing to report.	WEWR
"	July 8,	13.30 am	Lorry out to collect S.A.A. for OY there & to deliver to 6th M.G. Squadron & F.S.R.E. and 3rd Cav.	WEWR
"	9.7.16		Nothing to report. It Barrach goes on a course of instruction.	WEWR
"	10.7.16	2.0 pm	Three lorries out – one to D.J & E Batteries & other 85 Regt. H.E. 13 pdr & other 100 N°2 shell	WEWR
"	11.7.16	9.30 am	Six lorries out to OY. They collected ammunition from column – 85 pdr with N°1 gun ammunition to various and 100/N°2 gun ammunition to Column – Rem ord at Various. On OY gun in action – Teen one at OY Stn. & completely opening horses up to & is [undeciphered] 100 OY gun in action – All 95 pdr/gun with OY guns & 18" Balmorier & [undeciphered] & will motory horse to go [undeciphered]	WEWR
"	12.7.16	9.30 am	Six lorries take remainder of 85 forges to OY. One lorry detached to 2nd F.S.R.E.	WEWR
"	13.7.16	-	Nothing to report.	WEWR
"	14.7.16	8.0 am	Lorry out on fatigue work to Brewance Signals – Not to return to day.	WEWR
"	15.7.16	-	Nothing to report.	WEWR
"	16.7.16	12.30 am	Lorry returned from Divisional Signals and another lorry sent out. (8.0 am)	WEWR
"	17.7.16	8.0 am	Two more lorries detached to 2nd F.S.R.E. (See entry for 12.7.16).	WEWR
"	18.7.16	-	Nothing to report.	WEWR
"	19.7.16	-	Lorry out to 0.0.04 with S.A.A.	WEWR

WAR DIARY

~~INTELLIGENCE SUMMARY~~

(Erase heading not required.)

Army Form C. 2118

Instructions regarding War Diaries and Intelligence Summaries are contained in F. S. Regs., Part II. and the Staff Manual respectively. Title Pages will be prepared in manuscript.

Place	Date	Hour	Summary of Events and Information	Remarks and references to Appendices
HAZEBROUCK	20.7.16	8.30	Two lorries to OY to do work for the 5th Australian Division.	15/7/16
"	21.7.16	8.30	Two lorries out on Ordnance fatigue.	15/7/16
"	22.7.16		Nothing to report.	15/7/16
"	23.7.16	2.30	One lorry out with S.A.A. ammunition to A.D.O.S., 4th Cav Bgde and 5th 4th Cav. Squadron.	15/7/16 Return from Cavalry Cells 5th G.H.Q.
"	24.7.16, 25.7.16, 26.7.16, 27.7.16 & 28.7.16		Nothing to report.	15/7/16
"	29.7.16	2.30	Lorry to OY for ammunition (S.A.A.)	10/7/16
"	30.7.16		Capt Watson goes for course at S.G.H. & Ammunition Park.	15/7/16
"	31.7.16		Nothing to report.	15/7/16

August 1st 1916

P.W. Howard, Major A.S.C.
O.C. 2nd Cavalry Division Ammunition Park.

CONFIDENTIAL.

WAR DIARY OF

2nd CAV. DIV. AMMUNITION PARK

for August, 1916.

Vol. ~~XXIV~~

Army Form C. 2118

WAR DIARY
or
INTELLIGENCE SUMMARY
(Erase heading not required.)

Instructions regarding War Diaries and Intelligence Summaries are contained in F. S. Regs., Part II. and the Staff Manual respectively. Title Pages will be prepared in manuscript.

Place	Date	Hour	Summary of Events and Information	Remarks and references to Appendices
HAZEBROUCK	1.8.16	—	Nothing to report.	67201R
"	2.8.16	9.30	Lorry out to OY for ammunition.	67201R
"	3.8.16	9.0	Lorry out - to change grenades & collect new ones from OY.	67201R
"	4.8.16	9.15	Mills No's grenades changed on Cottonum Grand - Old grenades returned to _____ OY	67201R
"	5.8.16 and 6.8.16	—	Nothing to report.	67201R
"	7.8.16	9.30	Lorry out - to OY. to pick up ammunition & deliver to units	67201R
"	8.8.16	9.0	Two lorries out - on RE fatigue work.	67201R
"	9.8.16	9.30	Lorry out - to OY to pick up ammunition & deliver to units.	67201R
"	10.8.16	9.30	Lorry out - to OY to pick up ammunition - deliver to units.	67201R
"	11.8.16	8.0	Lorry out on RE fatigue work	67201R
"	12.8.16	—	Nothing to report.	67201R
"	13.8.16	2.30 pm	Changed over 2.3 of the working party at B.1. to 2.5	67201R
"	14.8.16 - 15.8.16 - 16.8.16 - 17.8.16	—	Nothing to report on this charge.	67201R
"	18.8.16	9.0 am	One lorry out - to OY farm to collect ammunition and one lorry to Tyr bras.	67201R
"	19.8.16	2.30 pm	Sent lorry out to OY farm to collect stores 3" ammunition Nissen. Three lorries on detachment - for fatigue RE are changed from another three lorries from Park.	67201R
"	20.8.16	—	Nothing to report.	67201R
"	21.8.16	9.30	Two lorries out issuing ammunition (S.A.A.) to 5 to Bgde unit.	67201R
"	22.8.16 to end of month.		Nothing to report.	67201R

Sd/W.H. Howard 1916

W.H. Howard
Major, A.S.C.

O.C. 2nd Cavalry Division Ammunition Park.

SECRET.

WAR   DIARY

of

ANMUNITION PARK, 2nd CAVALRY DIVISION

for September, 1916.

VOLUME XXV.
******

Army Form C. 2118

WAR DIARY
INTELLIGENCE SUMMARY
(Erase heading not required.)

2ND CAN. DIV'N AMMUNITION PARK

Place	Date	Hour	Summary of Events and Information	Remarks and references to Appendices
HAZEBROUCK	September 1st to 3rd	—	Nothing to report.	WZW76
"	4.9.16	—	Section Officers took their sections out on the march.	WZW76
"	5.9.16	—	Packing up for move tomorrow.	WZW76
ST VENANT	6.9.16		Started out from HAZEBROUCK 9.0 A.M arrived here at 4.0 P.M. Good billets on lower link of Officers found punctures.	WZW76
TANGRY	7.9.16 1.0 P.M		Started out from ST VENANT and proceeded via LILLERS, PERNES to TANGRY arr and S: 6'm/Kr: a very successful trip.	WZW76
VACQUERIETTE	9.16 10.30 AM		Started out & proceeded via FLEURY, WAVANS, FREGNOY and WAIL to VACQUERIETTE. A very good & successful run. depots went and arrived here 3.30.	WZW76
"	9.10.16	—	Rested all day and went in necessary returns.	WZW76
VILLERS L'HOPITAL	10.10.16 3.0 AM		Started out at 3.0 AM via WAIL BOFFLES & VILLERS - Successful run and very nice jolts.	WZW76
VIGNACOURT	11.10.16 5.30 AM		Started out at 5.30 AM via BERNAVILLE and arrived VIGNACOURT about 10 a.m. No Billets.	WZW76
NRLE NEUVILLE	12.10.16 10.30 AM		Started out and proceeded via AMIENS QUERRIEU to the point I.14 b.7.7.* arrived about 12 to NEUVE.	*Sht 62 D WZW76
"	13.10.16	—	Rests all day.	WZW76
NRLE CARCAILLOT Farm	14.10.16 9.0 AM		Started out & proceeded via LAHOUSSOYE and ALBERT to hour E.19 a central & Trapland Copses in the field. There will undoubtedly be trouble at we have bad weather.	*Sht 62 D WZW76
	2.30 PM		Drew 45,000 rounds of S.A.A from OV Railhead and delivered to Colincamps.	WZW76
"	15.10.16 7.30		On way out to refill with grenades after delivering to Colincamps. Horses 2200 from OC Railhead delivered 600 to 9004 and returned to Park 4.0 am 16/10 = Lorry DABBEVILLE for 2 Officers 26/10	WZW76
"	17.10.16 12.0		Lorry returned from ABBEVILLE. Lorry out for Canteen stores for 3rd Brig until.	WZW76

Army Form C. 2118

WAR DIARY
or
INTELLIGENCE SUMMARY
(Erase heading not required.)

Instructions regarding War Diaries and Intelligence Summaries are contained in F. S. Regs, Part II. and the Staff Manual respectively. Title Pages will be prepared in manuscript.

October 1st 1916

Place	Date	Hour	Summary of Events and Information	Remarks and references to Appendices
N° 12 GREATWOOD farm	1.9.16	9.30	Lorry to collect and deliver ammunition to O L Malheux	WSW
"	19/9 to 25/9		Nothing of importance to report. Lorries out on fatigues for Brigade Couriers	WSW
"	26.9.16 to 28.9.16		Twenty two lorries of park (all available) working on drawing ammunition from rail head A.10.b.3.0. * Much difficulty experienced owing to the bad weather and trouble of traffic - Started each morning from Park at 6.0 am and last lorry usually in by 2.0 am all cleared but 3 small loads by evening of 28.9.	× Albert road 1/4 across
"	29.9.16	5.0 am	Three lorries out to clean dump. Two lorries out for Canteen for 3rd Brigade	WSW
"	30.9.16	9.0 am 10.10 am	Lorry to AMIENS to purchase stores for 5th Cavalry Brigade. Proceeded to AMIENS myself to purchase workshop stores	WSW

W.W.Howard
Major AS.C
O.C. 2nd Cavalry Ammunition Park.

SECRET.

WAR DIARY

of

2nd CAVALRY DIVL. AMMUNITION PARK.

OCTOBER, 1916.

VOL. XXVI.

WAR DIARY
INTELLIGENCE SUMMARY
(Erase heading not required.)

AMMUNITION PARK 2nd CAV. DIV.

Army Form C. 2118

Place	Date	Hour	Summary of Events and Information	Remarks and references to Appendices
M^CARCAILLOT FARM	01·10·1916	—	Nothing to report —	※ E 18. 9. 5.5
"	2·10·16	8.0 a.m	One lorry out - to 2nd F.S. R.E.	
"	3·10·16	8.10 a.m	One lorry out - to O.C. for 10000 rds of S.A.A. - Delivered 6000 to 6th B^de.	
"	4·10·16	8.10 a.m	One lorry out - for grenades - drew 2000 rds S.A.A from D.L.	
"	5·10·16	7.30 a.m	One lorry out - to draw 37,000 rds S.A.A delivered 3000 to 12 S^qn 11,000 to R.S.G and 17,000 to D.A.C.	
		9.10 a.m	Two lorries out - to 5th B^de to go to A.M.T.E.N.S. for hurdles of cavalry Horses.	
"	6·10·16	—	Nothing to report.	
"	7·10·16	—	Nothing to report.	
NEBUIRE.	8·10·16	1·30 p.m	Left Park for Bruire - Reported to O.C.M.T. XV Corps - Great difficulty was experienced in getting the lorries out of the field in which they were parked - Owing to XIV Corps order that lorries were not to parked on the road. Parking ground there is much better. Total hrs covered by lorries 250.	About ½000 @ 0·29·c·9·9 "
"	9·10·16	8.0 a.m	Returned 446.000 S.A.A to 125th A.S.P. Trump - 1800 Shrapnel & 900 H.E. returned to 374th Siege Amm Trump - Drew 560 A, 500 yellow flares and 100 Rockets Red & Green from XIV Corps Branch and issued 60 to No 7 A.S.P & lorries 292 to 41st Div Grenade Branch and Rockets & 30 to Div Grenade Branch - Total hrs by lorries on the date	
"	10·10·16	7·30 a.m	Eighteen lorries out on Road repair - Three lorries drew 300 B.S.K & 300 R.P.S also 5 717 B/1000 flares and delivered flares and lights to 30th Div Grenade Branch. The B.S.K & B.P.S & 210th Brinel Art^y Branch - Three lorries delivered 204,000 S.A.A collected from XV corps Branch to 12th Div Grenade Branch - Total hrs 757.	
"	11·10·16	7·30 a.m	Twenty lorries out on Road fatigue - On completing fatigue they drew 480 B.P.S and 2575 B.S.R from corps Branch and delivered 1290 B.S.K to 210th Brinel Branch. This duty was not yet completed - Total hrs for the day 922.	

WAR DIARY
or
INTELLIGENCE SUMMARY
(Erase heading not required.)

Army Form C. 2118

Instructions regarding War Diaries and Intelligence Summaries are contained in F.S. Regs., Part II. and the Staff Manual respectively. Title Pages will be prepared in manuscript.

Place	Date	Hour	Summary of Events and Information	Remarks and references to Appendices
N° BVIRE	12.10.16	10.30 am	Duty of following lorry completed – Drew from O₂ Y 550 w.x. and delivered to 1st H.A.G. (18) 17 lorries out on road repair. Total mileage for the day 1052.	1st W.R.
"	13.10.16	7.30 am	19 lorries out on Road repair. On completion lorries were sent to assist 51st A.S.P. to clear Edgehill of Ammunition – Total miles covered by lorries the day 1342.	1st W.R.
"	14.10.16	7.30 am	15 lorries out on Road repair – Total miles covered 503.	1st W.R.
"	15.10.16	9.30 am / 8.30	15 lorries out to assist 51st A.S.P clearing a dump of ammunition from Edgehill. One lorry drew 4000 flares from Contre Druyh – 2000 delivered to 30 Divnl. Dump – N.C.O. failed to find 12 Divnl. Dump & returned. Total miles covered to day 1022.	1st W.R.
"	16.10.16	10.30 am	Lorry took 6000 Very lights and remaining 2000 flares and delivered both to 12th Divnl. Dump & also delivered to 41st Divnl. Dump by same lorry 272 H.I.S Cartridges were drawn from O.V.	1st W.R.
"	17.10.16	9.0 am	19 lorries out to assist 51st A.S.P. clear ammunition from OLD FRICOURT. Total distance 5352. one lorry drew twice flares.	1st W.R. / 1253 WR
"	18.10.16	11.0 am	20 lorries out. Drew from OLD FRICOURT 800 AX, 328 BX, 647 DX and 1528D and delivered to 62nd H.A.G. 455 DX and 898 D, to 18 H.A.G. 192 BX and 630 D and to the 41st Divisional Dump 800 AX and 328 BX. Total miles covered 1198. (All lorries not got returning from OLD Fricourt)	1st W.R.
"	19.10.16	5.0 am	Sent lorry in from yesterday job. Seven lorries drew 300 D and 706 DX from OLD FRICOURT and delivered to 62nd R.A.G. dump – Total mileage 967.	1st W.R.
"	20.10.16	6.30 am	12 lorries out to assist 14 A.S.C with ammunition – Total mileage 846.	1st W.R.
"	21.10.16	6.30	11 lorries on/out road repair. Total mileage covered by lorries 281 miles.	1st W.R.

1875 Wt. W593/826 1,000,000 4/15 J.B.C. & A. A.D.S.S./Forms/C. 2118.

Army Form C. 2118

WAR DIARY
of
INTELLIGENCE SUMMARY
(Erase heading not required.)

Instructions regarding War Diaries and Intelligence Summaries are contained in F.S. Regs., Part II. and the Staff Manual respectively. Title Pages will be prepared in manuscript.

Place	Date	Hour	Summary of Events and Information	Remarks and references to Appendices
BUIRE	22.10.16	4.30am	15 lorries out on Road Repairs - 1 lorry & tipper broke down out lorry to lorry park (out M. 945 km) - MT mileage 603.	W3WR
"	23.10.16	4.30am	10 lorry out on Road repair - 1 lorry out for fatigue for C.R.E. XV Corps - Two lorries & lorry tipper for FRICOURT. Lorry to PONT NOYELLES - 1 lorry & Train Wagon at RIBEMONT on fatigue. 6 lorries lorry out on R.E. fatigue. 6 lorries drew 1000 G and 1000 Q x from O.Z.Y. and delivered 720 G & 720 Q x. to 7450, 280 G Q & 280 Q x were handed over to No.8 Anti Aircraft section - Total mileage for day 767.	W3WR
"	24.10.16	7.0 am	8 lorries out on road repair - 4 lorries out to assist 1A.L 459 - Total mileage 507.	15 WR
"	25.10.16	6.0 am	12 lorries out on road repair. - Total mileage covered by lorries 521	15 WR
"	26.10.16	6.0 am	17 lorries out on road repair. - Total mileage 448.	16 WR
"	27.10.16	5.30 am	20 lorries out on various fatigues for C.R.E. XV Corps - 703 miles covered by very lorries today.	W3WR
"	28.10.16	7.0 am	12 lorries out on Road repair - Total distance covered by these lorries to day 442 miles.	15 WR
"	29.10.16		Park moved on a BERNACOURT, MEAULTE & MORLANCOURT to a point K.2.a.8.8. near VILLE, park moved complete.	Small G.I.D. W3WR
Nr. VILLE	30.10.16	8.0 am	Filled batteries up to establishment with exception of D Battery which were unable to take full establishment by account of damaged limber. E Batty took 388 Nx complete & 1 batty took 3 ff 832 N complete, F Batty took 218 NB of N to enable required when their limbers are repaired. 720 N and 360 N x and 1489 N - Park also has surplus 180 rounds N x due to D battery. - Park drew 3 1.2 N to complete establishment of S.A.A.	W3WR
"	31.10.16		Park drew 3 1.2 N to complete establishment - Seven lorries out of action on account of new types required.	W3WR

November 1st 1916.

LCW Thomson
Major R.G.A.
O.C. 3rd Cavalry Ammunition Park

SECRET.

WAR DIARY

OF

2nd CAVALRY DIVISIONAL AMMUNITION PARK.

NOVEMBER, 1916.

VOL. XXVII.

Confidential

WAR DIARY
of
2nd Cavalry Field Ambulance

From 1.11.16 to 30.11.16

WAR DIARY
INTELLIGENCE SUMMARY

(Erase heading not required.)

Army Form C. 2118

2nd Cavalry Divisional Ammunition Park

Place	Date	Hour	Summary of Events and Information	Remarks and references to Appendices
N*. VILLE	1st.15th. Nov. November.		Nothing to report	—
"	5.11.16.	10.30 a.m	Two lorries to D battery with ammunition - Batty took some but returned one load again as unable to take it.	WD25/6
"	6.11.16	—	Nothing to report	WD26/10
"	7.11.16	8.0 am	Lorry collected surplus bombs from units - Some ruffly found with detonators in them. Reported same to A.A. & Q.M.G. - Detached lorry to Q. Office for transport of their furniture	WD27/9
BOURDON	8.11.16	12.0 a.m	Left VILLE at mid-day & proceeded via AMIENS to BOURDON. Picked line for Pk. Night arrived here 6.30 p.m. after a successful run - First detached section two lorries to Q Office.	WD28/6
CHERIENNE	9.11.16	9.0 am	After interviewing A.A.&Q.M.G. I detached two lorries to Q office & proceeded to CHERIENNE. Park moved in two batches - first batch in Pk. and arrived at 2.0 p.m. - 2nd Convoy under Captain N/15 B.E.T arrived at 3.0 pm -	WD29/6
		4.30 pm	Lt. ROACH took five lorries back to BONNEY (Q officer) for the purpose of bringing officers bedding party from the new area.	—
"	10.11.16		Lt. ROACH and 5 lorries returned (last lorry in about 11.00 p.m.)	WD30/6 WD31/6
"	11.11.16 & 12.11.16		Nothing to report	WD32/6
"	13.11.16	9.30 am	Two lorries out on R.E. fatigue.	WD33/9
"	14.11.16	—	Nothing to report	WD34/9
"	16.11.16	8.0 am	Lorry on fatigue order of A.A. & Q.M.G. to Divisional Signals.	WD25/9
"	17.11.16	8.10 am	Two lorries deal with R.E 1 cartridge A.A & Q.M.G.	WD26/10
"	18.11.16 to 19.11.16		About 12 lorries out each day. 2nd. to R.E. (9 and F Squadron) for conveyance of material to billets	WD27/10 WD28/8

WAR DIARY

INTELLIGENCE SUMMARY

(Erase heading not required.)

Army Form C. 2118

Instructions regarding War Diaries and Intelligence Summaries are contained in F.S. Regs., Part II. and the Staff Manual respectively. Title Pages will be prepared in manuscript.

Place	Date	Hour	Summary of Events and Information	Remarks and references to Appendices
CHERIENNE	20-11-16	3.45 pm	Major General G.O.C. to Division inspected the lines & a Runner inspressed his satisfaction at the condition of things in the company	
"	20-11-16	8.0 am	12 lorries out to R.E. Issued fatigues to units of division	
"	21/11/16 to 24 1/11/16		Nothing to report - escort to lorries out each day for distribution of material to Divisional Troops in the Division by R.E.	
"	25-11-16	8.0 am	12 lorries out on R.E. fatigues. Your lorries out for ammunition - (3 for R.E. Ws and 1 Hour flour enfilades etc. - These were delivered to units.)	
"	26/11/16 to 27/11/16		5 m lorries out each day for 2nd F.S. R.E. (H Pain on leave from 26 1/11.)	
"	28-11-16	6.30 am	6 lorries out on Royal repairs - sent to French authorities. Two lorries lent to the R.E. (fatigues).	
"	29/11/16 and 30/11/16		5 lorries out each day on Royal repairs for French authorities/out 6.30 am returns 12.0 noon.	

December 1st 1916

W. W. Jones
Major A.S.C.
O.C. 2nd (Cavalry) Ammunition Park R.

CONFIDENTIAL.

WAR DIARY

of

2nd CAVALRY DIVISIONAL AMMUNITION PARK.

DECEMBER, 1916.

VOL. XXVIII.

Confidential

WAR DIARY
of
2nd Cav. Brigade HQ

From 1.12.16 to 31.12.16

Army Form C. 2118

WAR DIARY
of
INTELLIGENCE SUMMARY
(Erase heading not required.)

2nd Cavalry Divn Summary

Instructions regarding War Diaries and Intelligence Summaries are contained in F.S. Regs, Part II. and the Staff Manual respectively. Title Pages will be prepared in manuscript.

Place	Date	Hour	Summary of Events and Information	Remarks and references to Appendices
CHERIENNE	Dec 1st & 2nd		Six lorries out each day at 7.0 a.m to HESDIN for stone. There to various parts of divisional area for road repair.	
"	Dec 3rd	7.0 a.m	Two lorries to J Battery. Three lorries returned 4.0 p.m on 5th.	17W
"	Dec 4th 5 & 6th		Seven lorries out each day for Road Repairs as on 1st & 2nd	17W
"	Dec 7th	7.0 a.m	Six lorries out on road repair and seven out on R.E. work. Major Wadsforward goes on leave.	17W
"	Dec 8th, 9th, 10th		Six lorries out each day on road repair – 2nd Lt Gallacher in/unit employees held on change by Division.	17W
"	Dec 11th to Dec 16th		Eight lorries out each day on Stone fatigue.	17W
"	Dec 17th	8.15 a.m	Lorry with wheels for lighting St. POL.	17W
"	Dec 18th	7.0 a.m	7 lorries out for Road Repair. Major Stewart returns off leave.	
"	Dec 19th to Dec 22nd		7 lorries out each day on Road Repair. 2nd Lt Wight goes on leave Dec 2nd – 10th W.	Out 7.0 a.m each day
"	Dec 24th	7.45 a.m	Lorry out to R.E. returned 9.25 p.m	17W
"	Dec 25th	—	Nothing to report.	
"	Dec 26th	6.30 a.m	Four lorries out on Stone fatigue	17W
"	Dec 27th	6.35 a.m	Nine lorries out on Stone fatigue and two lorries out on R.E. fatigue	17W
"	Dec 28th	6.30 a.m	Ten lorries out on 6 Cavalry fatigue and four lorries out on R.E. fatigue	17W
"	Dec 29th	6.30 a.m 9.30 a.m	Seven lorries out on Stone fatigue. One lorry out with 6 A.K. regiments of 4 D & 5 a B.Gdes	
"	Dec 30th	6.30 a.m	Seven lorries out on Stone fatigue – one lorry to R.E. and one lorry out to Divisional signals	17W
"	Dec 31st	6.30 a.m	One lorry out to divisional signals	17W

January 1st 1917.

W.Watsonwell – Major RE
O.C. 2nd Cavalry Ammunition Park

CONFIDENTIAL.

WAR DIARY

of

2nd CAVALRY DIVISIONAL AMMUNITION PARK.

JANUARY, 1917.

VOL. XXIX.

Confidential.

War Diary
of.
2nd C.A.N. Ammⁿ Park.

From. 1- 1- 17 to 31- 1- 17

WAR DIARY or INTELLIGENCE SUMMARY

Army Form C. 2118

(Erase heading not required.)

Place	Date	Hour	Summary of Events and Information	Remarks and references to Appendices
CHERISIENNE	1-1-17	6.30	One lorry for stores and three lorries for the R.E. (3rd F.S.)	
"	2-1-17	3.11-17	Fourteen lorries out on Stone Fatigue each day. 63 am	
"	4-1-17	6.30am	7 lorries for Road metal (stone) and six lorries for the R.E.	
"	5-1-17	6-1-17	13 lorries out on stone work each day at 6.30 am.	
"	7-1-17	7.30am	6 lorries out to the R.E. going on manoeuvres – 10 lorries out to Pioneer Battalion	
"	8-1-17	7.30am	6 lorries out to R.E. and four out on Road mending – One out to collect ammunition from 1st 2nd D.N. at 2.0 pm.	
"	9-1-17 10-1-17		6 lorries out to R.E. each day (out at 8.30 am hours at 4.30 hrs – On 9th 9th of month 5 drivers & 5 gunners of Pioneer Battalion to surplus gunners to pose.	
"	11-1-17 12-1-17		Three lorries out each day on R.E. work. On 11th Lt Baker reported for duty to this office vice Lt ROACH under orders for 46th F.S.C. On 12th Lt. Gallichan returns off leave.	
"	13-1-17	9.10 am	Lt. ROACH leaves Park for 46th S.C. reported same to 2C/45c in accordance with instructions.	
"	Jan 15 & 17		Six lorries out each day to the R.E. at 7.30 am.	
"	18-1-17	—	Nothing to report.	
"	19-1-17	—	Six lorries out to 2nd F.S. R.E. and one lorry out with ammunition to unit.	
"	20-1-17 to 23-1-17		Two lorries out each day to 3rd F.S. R.E. at 7.30 am – On 23rd one lorry out to supply	
"	24-1-17 25-1-17		Nothing to report.	
"	26-1-19	7.30am	Four lorries out to R.E. & one delivering ammunition to various units	
"	27-1-17 28-1-17		Three lorries out to F.R.E. on 27th and one out on 28th	
"	29-1-17 30-1-17		Nothing to report.	
"	31-1-17	4.30 pm	ADSS & T visited had to found everything correct.	

February 1st/2/1917

[signature] Major A.S.C.
OC. 2nd Cavalry Ammunition Park

CONFIDENTIAL.

Vol 29

WAR   DIARY

of

2nd CAVALRY DIVISIONAL AMMUNITION PARK.

FEBRUARY, 1917.
VOL. XXX.

****

WAR DIARY
INTELLIGENCE SUMMARY

(Erase heading not required.)

Army Form C. 2118

Instructions regarding War Diaries and Intelligence Summaries are contained in F.S. Regs., Part II. and the Staff Manual respectively. Title Pages will be prepared in manuscript.

Place	Date	Hour	Summary of Events and Information	Remarks and references to Appendices
CHAMIENNE	1·2·17	—	Nothing to report	
"	2·2·17	9 a.m	Lorry out to Lyr press - One lorry out to deliver ammunition - This is done every Fridays	
"	3·2·17 and 4·2·17		Nothing to report.	
"	5·2·17	6·20 am	Two lorries out to collect coal for 4th & 5th Bdes - 8·50 am one lorry return to the R.E	
"		7·0 pm	One lorry to HD Bgts for ammunition.	
"	6·2·17 & 7·2·17		Nothing to report.	
"	8·2·17	11·30	Turned over the Small Arm ammunition of the Column - 5 lorries used.	
"	9·2·17	—	Nothing to report.	
"	10·2·17	7·30 am	Two lorries lent to R.E.	
"	11·2·17 & 17·2·17		Nothing to report.	
"	18·2·17	8·30 am	Two lorries out to R.E.	
"	19·2·17 & 26·2·17		Nothing to report.	
"	27·2·17	8·0 am	9 lorries out all lent to 4, 5 Bgds. 2 lorries, 3 each regiment. Lorries broken down and this started.	
GUIGNY	28·2·17		Park moves to GUIGNY. Lorries unable to park in village ordered to put horses in village near GUIGNY on high road as given too park, but horses had to take them nearer HESDIN. Park is at Mourier 2½ miles from Office. are quite comfortable. ABBEVILLE road.	

March 1st 1917.

b.j.w. Kenton
Capt. I.M. & Com. Officer Park.

CONFIDENTIAL.

Vol 30

WAR   DIARY

of

2nd CAVALRY DIVISIONAL AMMUNITION PARK.

MARCH, 1917.

VOL.XXXI.

Confidential.

WAR DIARY.
of
2nd Cav: Bgde Hqrs.

From 1.3.17 to 31.3.17

WAR DIARY
or
INTELLIGENCE SUMMARY
(Erase heading not required.)

Army Form C. 2118

Instructions regarding War Diaries and Intelligence Summaries are contained in F.S. Regs., Part II. and the Staff Manual respectively. Title Pages will be prepared in manuscript.

Place	Date	Hour	Summary of Events and Information	Remarks and references to Appendices
GUIGNY	1.3.17	8.0 am	Completed the move from CAERIE NNE GUIGNY	
"	2.3.17	8.0 am	6" lorries out changing ammunition for J Battery WWR	
"	3.3.17 & 5.3.17		Nothing to report. DSWR	
WADICOURT	6.3.17	9.0 am	Park moves to WADICOURT decided to go via LE BOISLE and CRECY arrived about 11.30 am. DSWR	
"	7.3.17 & 11.3.17		Nothing to report. DSWR	
"	12.3.17	8.30 am	One lorry out to each Battery on changing ammunition. DSWR	
"	13.3.17 & 14.3.17		Nothing to report. DSWR	
"	15.3.17	10.0 am	Seven lorries out to BOULOGNE to dump 95 fused N returns was defective. this was dumped but lorries had to go on to AUDRECQ & fill up with 100 fused N. Returned 16 Feb. DSWR	
"	16.3.17	4.30 pm	Received instructions to forming Ammunition dumps in forward area from Cavalry Corps. DSWR	
"	17.3.17	—	Nothing to report Prepared for moving off tomorrow WWR	
TINCQUES	18.3.17	—	Left WADICOURT at 8.30 and arrived at ST POL at 1.0 pm - Picked 5 lorries from the Supply Column sent to fill the Park - loads to back towards also loads on a lorry. St officer & 50 men for work on dump - Lt BRADLEY reported with 32 men for loading the Railhead. Arrived TINCQUES 3.0 pm Lorries proceeded to dump & were off loaded lorries returned 3.45 am. Both lorries & Northern party of 50 men & 10 gunners at dump night.	WWR

1875 Wt. W501/826 1,000,000 4/15 J.B.C. & A. A.D.S.S./Forms/C. 2118.

WAR DIARY
or
INTELLIGENCE SUMMARY

(Erase heading not required.)

Army Form C. 2118

Instructions regarding War Diaries and Intelligence Summaries are contained in F. S. Regs., Part II. and the Staff Manual respectively. Title Pages will be printed in manuscript.

Place	Date	Hour	Summary of Events and Information	Remarks and references to Appendix
TINCQUES	19.3.17	—	Nothing to report - men rested & bathed. Found & buried horses. NWM	
"	20.3.17 to 25.3.17	15	The horses carried up ammunition each night after training each day. No horses were taken later at gun dump. The work was completed on the 24-3-17 with the exception of 3 in. Hotchkiss - The workmen (men with lorries) were put on the night of 25th - 26th and the Gallactier with them and an NCO were put in charge of the dump. NWM	
WADICOURT	26.3.17	—	Russ returned to WADICOURT carrying about 30 km after a successful run. 3 left unit today up at OPB. to take at the 500 3 in Hotchkiss when in should arrive at Ref then down the line. NWM	
"	27.3.17	—	Nothing to report.	
"	28.3.17	—	Put two lorries DOCAGE in the convoy at PENDE. NWM	
"	29.3.17	—	Lorry usual work carrots to Royal S.O.S. NWM	
"	30.3.17 11.30am		Two lorries left for about 3 days to take working parties to forward areas. NWM	
"	31.3.17 9.10am		Four lorries exchanged 580 effective 13 hr A.F. forwards with Colonne. NWM	

April 1st 1917.

[Signed] M. W. Hoofer(?) Major
O.C. 2nd Corps Heavy Arty.

Confidential.

WAR DIARY.
of
2nd Cav: Amm'n Pk

From 1.3.17. to 31.3.17.

CONFIDENTIAL.

WAR DIARY

of

2nd CAVALRY DIVISIONAL AMMUNITION PARK.

VOL. XXXII.

APRIL, 1917.

Confidential

WAR DIARY

of

2' Cav. Bmtn Bk

From 1.4.'17 to 30.4.'17

WAR DIARY
or
INTELLIGENCE SUMMARY

Army Form C. 2118

(Erase heading not required.)

Instructions regarding War Diaries and Intelligence Summaries are contained in F. S. Regs., Part II. and the Staff Manual respectively. Title Pages will be prepared in manuscript.

Place	Date	Hour	Summary of Events and Information	Remarks and references to Appendices
MAUDICOURT	1-4-17	5.30am / 7.00am	Two lorries to carry fatigue party & forward cart for carrying traps returned 3.45 pm 14/17. Two lorries out with ammunition.	
"	2-4-17	6.30am / 6.30am	Four lorries out to BOULOGNE & two ammunition returned 8.0 pm. One lorry out to signals returned at 7.0 pm.	
"	3-4-17	8.0am	Two vehicles lorries out to various units on Divisional fatigues.	
"	4-4-17	6.15am	Two lorries to Boulogne for ammunition. All ammunition sent to M.A.H.T. 30 on Divisional fatigues.	
"	5-4-17 and 6-4-17		Nothing to report. Save 12 lorries out on fatigue & Lorry horses may - Lime lorry returned sometime during night at 6.4.17 - 7-4-17.	
RACECOURT	7-4-17 to 8-4-17		Remaining lorries with park unit moved on the 7th & 8.4.17. Arrived after a good run - On the 8th the park head quarters moved to RACECOURT and the Parks came directly under the orders of infantry Corps.	
"	9-4-17	2.0 pm	Park sent 13 lorries to find of units ammunition & complete units reserve. at D.A.P. R.	
"	10-4-17 to 15-4-17		Nothing to report. Lorries inspected on 15th by B.G. T.I. all lorries and ammunition settled in order.	
"	16-4-17		Two lorries out for ammunition, the remainder still on Divisional fatigues.	

WAR DIARY
or
INTELLIGENCE SUMMARY

(Erase heading not required.)

Army Form C. 2118

Place	Date	Hour	Summary of Events and Information	Remarks and references to Appendices
ROLLIECOURT	17-4-17	—	Nothing to report.	
"	19-4-17	—	All arrived. Lorries out on Divisional fatigue. Three lorries returned at different times on 17" & 19-4-17.	WAR
"	19-4-17	noon	Three lorries out to ARRAS to hill to their Bo-dump.	WAR
HENU	20-4-17 12 noon	Coy. moved to HENU.		WAR
"	21-4-17 11-30 am	14 lorries out on divisional fatigue under H.Q. 91st/3.	WAR
"	22-4-17 11-0 am	9 lorries out to AOLLECOURT to pick up dumped ammunition. Two lorries with ammunition Brigade - and two lorries D.R.E.	WAR
"	23-4-17	—	Nothing to report.	
"	24-4-17 7-45 am	Two lorries to the R.E. #1 2-30 km Lorries out on coal fatigue. Two lorries to divisional & Cogone.	WAR
"	25-4-17 7-45am	Four lorries out on R.E. fatigue - two lorries out to the 3rd & 9th Brigades.	WAR
"	26-4-17 7-15 am	Four lorries out on R.E. fatigue.	WAR
"	27-4-17 7-45	Four lorries out on R.E. fatigue & some lorry carrying ammunition to Batteries under.	WAR
"	28-4-17 7-45	Four lorries D.R.E. Two lorries to Divisional H.Q. A.13 and others.	WAR
"	29-4-17 7-45	Four lorries D.R.E. 2 lorries to Rail - under divisional orders for carriage of troops and four lorries for Road mounting to the XVIII Corps.	WAR
"	30-4-17 7-45	Four lorries D.R.E. and four lorries to the XVIII Corps for road repairing.	WAR

May 1st 1917

W. M. Brown
Major RA
O.C. 2nd Cavalry Ammunition Park.

Confidential.

WAR DIARY
of.
2nd Cav. Division G.S.

From 1-4-17 to 30-4-17.

Vol 32

Confidential

WAR DIARY
of
2nd Cav. Ammunition Pk

from 1.5.17 to 31.5.17

Army Form C. 2118

WAR DIARY
or
INTELLIGENCE SUMMARY
(Erase heading not required.)

Instructions regarding War Diaries and Intelligence Summaries are contained in F. S. Regs., Part II. and the Staff Manual respectively. Title Pages will be prepared in manuscript.

Place	Date	Hour	Summary of Events and Information	Remarks and references to Appendices
HENU	1-5-17	7.45	Four lorries out on RE fatigues and 4 lorries out on road mending (for the RMS) Corps Group	
"	2-5-17	7.45	Six lorries on RE work and 4 lorries on Stone fatigues	
"	3-5-17	7.0 / 8.0am	12 lorries out on RE work	
"	4-5-17	6-5-17	Four lorries out on RE work & four lorries on Stone fatigues work Party	
"	8-5-17 / 10-5-17		Four lorries on Stone fatigues	
"	11-5-17 12-5-17	4.05 / 8.0	One lorry and Battery Armourer - 15 lorries out for carrying tiles of Frouville Wilton & Short, 1st Wiltshire Bat. on Leave.	
FOUILLOY	13-5-17	11.0am	Park moved from HENU to FOUILLOY after a successful run.	
LONGAVESNES	14-5-17		Park moved from FOUILLOY & LONGAVESNES. (Successful run)	
"	15-5-17	7.0am	Lighter lorries to continue to fetch at... and returned on the morning of 16-5-17	
"	16-5-17	6-15 / 17	Nothing to report	
"	17-5-17	9.0am	Eight lorries out on Brigade fatigues - Major WENHAM AR ADSMT commanded of Corps Ammunition Parks	
"	20-5-17	6.0am	Three lorries out on ammunition to Aff-Corps Group	
TINCOURT	21-5-17	11.0am	Park moved to TINCOURT. Capt AUSBET left aff at LONGAVESNES & was Town Major	

1875   Wt. W593/826   1,000,000   4/15   J.B.C. & A.   A.D.S.S./Forms/C. 2118.

WAR DIARY
or
INTELLIGENCE SUMMARY

(Erase heading not required.)

Army Form C. 2118

Place	Date	Hour	Summary of Events and Information	Remarks and references to Appendices
TINCOURT	22/5/17		Twelve lorries on ammunition and 3 on extraneous duties.	WD
"	23/5/17		Ten lorries on ammunition and 4 on extraneous duties	WD
"	25/5/17		All available lorries (18) out on extraneous duties.	WD
"	26/5/17		Eleven lorries out on ammunition and 11 lorries out on extraneous duties	WD
"	26/5/17		Four lorries out on ammunition less the available 16) on extraneous duties	WD
"	27/5/17		Twenty three lorries out on extraneous duties.	
"	27/5/17		Twenty one lorries out on extraneous duties (two on two /summary)	WD
"	28/5/17		Eight lorries out on Ammunition and two on extraneous duties	WD
"	29/5/17		Fifteen lorries out on Ammunition and one on extraneous duty	WD
"	30/5/17		Fifteen lorries out on extraneous duties.	WD
"	31/5/17		One lorry out on Ammunition and one on extraneous duty	WD

for O.C. 3rd Can A.S.C

Confidential

WAR DIARY
of
2nd Cav Remounts Dept

Lucknow 1.3.17 to 31.3.17

Vol 33

Confidential

WAR DIARY.
of
2nd Cavalry Remount Park.

from 1st June 1917 to 30th June 1917.

(Vol:-)

WAR DIARY
or
INTELLIGENCE SUMMARY

(Erase heading not required.)

Army Form C. 2118

Place	Date	Hour	Summary of Events and Information	Remarks and references to Appendices
TINCOURT	1/6/17	—	Thirteen lorries out on Extraneous duty. Three lorries on Ammunition duty	
"	2/6/17	—	Twelve lorries on Extraneous duty. Four lorries on Ammunition duty.	10 T.M.
"	3/6/17	—	Thirteen lorries on Extraneous duty.	10 T.M.
"	4/6/17	—	Eleven lorries on Ammunition duty. Seven do two journeys. Seventeen lorries out on Extraneous duty.	10 T.M.
"	5/6/17	—	Six lorries out on Extraneous duty. Nine lorries out on Ammunition duty.	10 T.M.
"	6/6/17	—	Eleven lorries out on Extraneous duty. One lorry out on Ammunition duty.	10 T.M.
"	7/6/17	—	Nineteen lorries out on Extraneous duty.	10 T.M.
"	8/6/17	—	Fifteen lorries out on Extraneous duty.	10 T.M.
"	9/6/17	—	Twenty lorries out on Extraneous duty. Two lorries out on Ammunition duty.	10 T.M.
"	10/6/17	—	Six lorries out on Extraneous duty. Nine lorries out on Ammunition duty.	10 T.M.
"	11/6/17	—	Nineteen lorries out on Extraneous duty. Eight lorries out on Ammunition duty. Five do two journeys	10 T.M.
"	12/6/17	—	Seventeen lorries out on Extraneous duty.	10 T.M.
"	13/6/17	—	Eleven lorries out on Extraneous duty. Nine lorries out on Ammunition.	10 T.M.

Army Form C. 2118

WAR DIARY
or
INTELLIGENCE SUMMARY
(Erase heading not required.)

Instructions regarding War Diaries and Intelligence Summaries are contained in F. S. Regs., Part II. and the Staff Manual respectively. Title Pages will be prepared in manuscript.

Place	Date	Hour	Summary of Events and Information	Remarks and references to Appendices
TINCOURT	14/6/17	—	Thirteen lorries out on Refreneous duty	W.T.R.
"	15/6/17	—	Two lorries out on Refreneous duty. Twelve lorries out on Ammunition duty	W.T.R.
"	16/6/17	—	Fifteen lorries out on Refreneous duty. Six lorries out on Ammunition duty	W.T.R.
"	17/6/17	—	Fifteen lorries out on Refreneous duty	W.T.R.
"	18/6/17	—	Twelve lorries out on Refreneous duty. Four lorries out on Ammunition duty	W.T.R.
"	19/6/17	—	Six lorries out on Refreneous duty	W.T.R.
"	20/6/17	—	Twelve lorries out on Ammunition duty. Twelve lorries out on Refreneous duty. Two lorries out on Ammunition duty	W.T.R.
"	21/6/17	—	Seventeen lorries out on Refreneous duty	W.T.R.
"	22/6/17	—	Thirteen lorries out on Refreneous duty	W.T.R.
"	23/6/17	—	Fifteen lorries out on Refreneous duty	W.T.R.
"	24/6/17	—	Fifteen lorries out on Ammunition duty	W.T.R.
"	25/6/17	—	Thirteen lorries out on Ammunition duty	W.T.R.
"	26/6/17	—	Twelve lorries out on Refreneous duty. Three lorries out on Ammunition duty.	W.T.R.

Army Form C. 2118

WAR DIARY
or
INTELLIGENCE SUMMARY

(Erase heading not required.)

Instructions regarding War Diaries and Intelligence Summaries are contained in F.S. Regs., Part II. and the Staff Manual respectively. Title Pages will be prepared in manuscript.

Place	Date	Hour	Summary of Events and Information	Remarks and references to Appendices
TINCOURT	27/6/17	—	Seven lorries out on Ammunition duty. Three lorries out on Ammunition duty.	W.Sn.
"	28/6/17	—	Eight lorries out on Ammunition duty. Eleven lorries out on Ammunition duty.	W.Sn.
"	29/6/17	—	Fourteen lorries out on Ammunition duty. One lorry out on Ammunition duty.	W.Sn.
"	30/6/17	—	Eight lorries out on Ammunition duty. Eleven lorries out on Ammunition duty.	W.Sn.

10 J Market Cottage

for Officer Commanding
2nd Cavalry Ammunition Park

1/7/7

Confidential

WAR DIARY
of
2nd Cavalry Brigade from 1st to 30th June 1917.

Kking. 1st June 1917

(Vol:-)

Confidential.

WAR DIARY.
of
2nd Cav: Bnde "A"

From 1.4.14 to 31.4.14

Army Form C. 2118

WAR DIARY
or
INTELLIGENCE SUMMARY
(Erase heading not required.)

Instructions regarding War Diaries and Intelligence Summaries are contained in F. S. Regs., Part II. and the Staff Manual respectively. Title Pages will be prepared in manuscript.

Place	Date	Hour	Summary of Events and Information	Remarks and references to Appendices
TINCOURT	1/7/17	—	Fourteen lorries out on Extraneous Duty	W.D.R.
"	2/7/17	—	Seven lorries out on Ammunition Duty. Twelve lorries out on Extraneous Duty.	W.D.R.
"	3/7/17	—	Nineteen lorries out on Extraneous Duty	W.D.R.
"	4/7/17	—	Twelve lorries out on Ammunition Duty. Eight lorries out on Extraneous Duty	W.D.R.
"	5/7/17	—	Seventeen lorries out on Extraneous Duty	W.D.R.
"	6/7/17	—	Six lorries out on Ammunition Duty. Twelve lorries out on Extraneous Duty	W.D.R.
"	7/7/17	—	Sixteen lorries out on Ammunition Duty. One lorry out on Extraneous Duty	W.D.R.
"	8/7/17	—	Thirteen lorries out on Extraneous Duty	W.D.R.
"	9/7/17	—	Eleven lorries out on Ammunition Duty. Eight lorries out on Extraneous Duty	W.D.R.

Army Form C. 2118

WAR DIARY
or
INTELLIGENCE SUMMARY
(Erase heading not required.)

Instructions regarding War Diaries and Intelligence Summaries are contained in F.S. Regs., Part II and the Staff Manual respectively. Title Pages will be prepared in manuscript.

Place	Date	Hour	Summary of Events and Information	Remarks and references to Appendices
TINCOURT	10.7.17		Cavalry Corps Ammunition Parks having been disbanded Major W.E.W. HOWARD & guns reserves comm and of the Park. No lorries out.	WJWH
"	11.7.17	9.30 am / 4.30 pm	9 lorries out. To load up ammunition as X.V. 1752 N and 948 NX. 6 lorries out. To collect empties and return to X.V.	WJWH
"	12.7.17	9.20 am / 10.30 am	4 lorries out on various extraneous duties. 5 lorries out on ammunition.	WJWH
"	13.7.17	—	Nothing to report.	WJWH
GOUY - E.W. TERNOIS	14.7.17 / 15.7.17	9.20 am	Park moves from TINCOURT to GOUY. Sleeping on night of 14th/15th at FRANVILLERS 15.7.17 Lieut Baker-Notson on leave to FRANCE. (6 days)	WJWH
GOUY	16.7.17	9.0 am	Six lorries out on fatigue - (Yeons troughs)	
"	17.7.17	7.45 am	Three lorries out on R.E. fatigue. Lt GALLAHER on leave to England (10 days)	WJWH
"	18.7.17	6.0 am	One lorry out for 4th A.G.B. - long journey & uncertain	WJWH
"	19.7.17	7.30 am	Three lorries out for R.E. fatigue and four lorries out on various duties at different times.	WJWH
"	20.7.17	7.30 am	Two lorries out on R.E. fatigue	WJWH
"	21.7.17	6.45	Three lorries on R E fatigue and three lorries on other extraneous duties	WJWH
"	23.7.17	7.45	Two lorries out to R.E. and one to D & D.S. — Note. Nothing to report on 22 nd	WJWH
"	24.7.17	7.45	Three lorries to R E and one lorry to Sembury Section Lt BAKER back from leave in France	WJWH

WAR DIARY
or
INTELLIGENCE SUMMARY

(Erase heading not required.)

Army Form C. 2118

Place	Date	Hour	Summary of Events and Information	Remarks and references to Appendices
GOUY	25.7.17	8.0am	One lorry for recruiting section & One lorry for 3rd Brigade and one lorry to A.S. Office.	135WB
"	26.7.17	8.0am	Three lorries out on various labourers duties.	135WB
"	27.7.17	6.15am	10 lorries out for conveyance of troops to Horse Show and various labourers duties.	135WB
"	28.7.17	6.15	10 lorries out for conveyance of troops to Horse Show.	135WB
"	29.7.17	10.30am	I-W15H-T 105h shell (13 h-) section to near BETHUNE E.16.c.o.6 Lt GALLACHIER accompanied him - the convoid Issue at 1.40pm after a good run. Attached to 36 A.S.P.	135WB
"	30.7.17	8.0am	One lorry out- D.O.P. for 60000 rds of S.A.A. ammunition. Two lorries out Dulin in this Coy on extraneous duties.	135WB
"	31.7.17	9.0am	One lorry out of San. Section and one for 2nd F.S.R.E.	135WB

July 31st 1917.

B.W. Howard
Major A.S.C.
O.C. No 1 Cavalry Ammunition Park.

Confidential.

WAR DIARY.

of

No. 1 Section RE

From 1.4.14 to 31.4.14

WA 35

Confidential.
War Diary.
of.
No. 2 Cavalry Ammunition Park

From 1. 8. 14. to. 31. 8. 14.

No. 2
CAVALRY
AMMUNITION PARK.
No. A00/26
31. 8. 17

Army Form C. 2118

WAR DIARY
or
INTELLIGENCE SUMMARY
(Erase heading not required.)

Instructions regarding War Diaries and Intelligence Summaries are contained in F.S. Regs., Part II. and the Staff Manual respectively. Title Pages will be prepared in manuscript.

Place	Date	Hour	Summary of Events and Information	Remarks and references to Appendices
GOUY-EN-TERNOIS	1-8-17	4.0 pm	One lorry out to Tyre tubes - Returned 4.0 pm next day.	
"	2-8-17	3-8-17	Nothing to report. Jr. B.M. Baker goes on leave on 2nd.	
"	4-8-17	7.30 am	Four lorries out on RE fatigue.	
"	5-8-17	7.30 am	One lorry to R.E.	
"	6-8-17	7.0 am	One lorry to Signals and Cav. Bde.	
"	7-8-17	9.0 am	Lorry sent to No 4 R Sanitary Section.	
"	8-8-17	7.10 am	Two lorries sent to A.O.O.M. One lorry returned 11.0 pm. The other at 8.0 pm on 9-8-17.	
"	9-8-17	13-8-17	Nothing to report. Sent out lorry out each day to R.E. at 7.30 am. Capt Niblett went on leave on 10-8-17. 8.45am	
"	14-8-17	10.10 am	Lorry to O.R.D. for green leaves. Returned 12.0 noon 15/8/17.	
"	15-8-17	7.30 am	One lorry to 3rd F.S. R.E.	
"	16-8-17	8.10 am	One lorry to Beauville to attach infantry for 2nd 3rd and 1st Divisions.	
"	17-8-17		Nothing to report.	
"	18-8-17	5-45 am	Lorry to 4/D Division for fatigue. Jr. Baker returns off leave.	
"	19-8-17		Nothing to report.	
"	20-8-17	7.30 am	Jr. Wight with 13 lorry section returns off detachment.	
"	21-8-17	7.0 am	Two lorries to 3rd F.S. R.E. Capt NIBLETT Returns off leave.	
"	22-8-17	8.45 AM	Three lorries sent to Town Major of GOUY.	
"	23-8-17	7.15 am 11.30 am	Two lorries sent to R.E. Bower shampad 13 hr from SIGNY-ST FISCHER and delivered 1584 rounds to loterinary @ 360 rds to D. Section	

1875 Wt. W50/1826 1,000,000 4/15 J.B.C. & A. A.D.S.S./Forms/C. 2118.

WAR DIARY
or
INTELLIGENCE SUMMARY

(Erase heading not required.)

Army Form C. 2118

Place	Date	Hour	Summary of Events and Information	Remarks and references to Appendices
GUOY-EN-TERNOIS	24-8-17	8.0 a.m.	Ten lorries out to draw ammunition from VALHEUREUX. Delivered 960 rounds of A.A. to J & E Battys and 300 rounds to D Batty. - 42 rounds of N.K. to J Batty.	WW
		7.15 p.m.	Two lorries out to 2nd F.S. R.E.	
"	25-8-17 & 28-8-17		Nothing to report.	WW
"	29-8-17	6.30 a.m.	8 lorries out for 2nd F.S. R.E.	
		11.30 a.m.	Two lorries out to draw SAA from BAINVILLE.	WW
"	30-8-17	8.10 a.m.	Two lorries deliver SAA to Columns	
		7.15 p.m.	One lorry to 2nd F.S. R.E.	WW
"	31-8-17	6.30 a.m.	One lorry to XI Brigade for fatigue	
		7.30 a.m.	Three lorries to D Bn R.E.	WW
		8.30 a.m.	One lorry with Ammunition to Columns — exchanging 80 rounds of N. forward deflection.	

September 1st 1917.

L.W. Howard
Major RSE
OC No 2 Cavalry Ammunition Park.

Army Form C. 2118

WAR DIARY
or
INTELLIGENCE SUMMARY
(Erase heading not required.)

Instructions regarding War Diaries and Intelligence Summaries are contained in F.S. Regs., Part II. and the Staff Manual respectively. Title Pages will be prepared in manuscript.

Place	Date	Hour	Summary of Events and Information	Remarks and references to Appendices
Béthune	17.8.17	7 p.m.	Lorry Park at E1 b c.o.b moved position for a front 2 miles distant owing to enemy shelling road on which lorries were parked. Return on to position original late at 10 p.m.	
BETHUNE	18.8.17	7 p.m.	Lieut. Wright & 10 lorries moved for Roadwork 12 on division of 19th inf. Bde. Returned at 6 a.m. 19th	
			Moved to Aix Noulette south of Souchez arriving at 9 a.m. Unit at work at —	
	19.8.17		6 p.m. on the 19th inst.	
	20.8.17	11 a.m.	Five lorries moved to 1st Aust Div. Amm. station — 1205 Q.4 M.Y. Return to Park at 4.30	
			— 6 Lt. D.O.5 & at over 1.31 R.6.6 M.Y. 11 p.m.	
GOUY-EN-TERNOIS	20.8.17	4 p.m.	Lieut. Wright & unit Eleven lorries & 19.8.17 at C1 d M.Y. Return to Park H.O. orders were received from D.G.1.27 Corps Park. Arrived at Park 7 p.m.	

WAR DIARY
or
INTELLIGENCE SUMMARY

(Erase heading not required.)

Army Form C. 2118

Place	Date	Hour	Summary of Events and Information	Remarks and references to Appendices
Fosseux	29.7.17	10 a.m	Lieut. M. Whyte & 2nd Lt. R. Humphris left Park with 2 carts, 11 lorries carrying 17.5.2 Fld. N. + 94.8 Fld. N.X. also to A.T.A.T.O.1st Corps at 1.40 p.m. afterwards attached to 4 B.W. Lorries Butlers Half M.T.	Map 36B E.16.a.6
	30.7.17	2 p.m	1752 M.M.N.X. Lorries over to O.4; 14 Fld. No 2 drwn at E30C.6.6.	Map 36B
		5½ m	Lieut. A. Whyte proceed to tan. Corps N. 2 for duty.	M.W.
Béthune		6 p.m	10 old + 9 m.w. of Park attached to 1st Corps drwn for duty	M.W.
Béthune	31.7.17		Nil	
	1.8.17		Nil	
	2.8.17		Nil	
	3.8.17		Nil	
	4.8.17		Nil	
	5.8.17	7 p.m	6 lorries proceed to bailly-our-la-Lys & Merris to Imag. and anti troops. Return to Park at 5 p.m. en route O.35.6 central	Map 36B M.W.
	6.8.17		Nil	
	11.8.17		Nil	
Béthune	12.8.17	7 a.m	5 lorries with M.G.O. report for duty to Roads Officer 1st Corps are attached till further orders for Mairead Bypass, Vermin E.29.63.3.	M.W.
Béthune	14.8.17	9 p.m	Four lorries report to the O.C. 1st Corps Siege Park. Returning at 1 a.m. ca 15 M knot	M.W.
	15.8.17		Nil	
	15.8.17	10 a.m	Five lorries report to 1st Reg.Section railhead to clear train	M.W.
		7.30 pm	Six lorries proceed to 1st Corps dump to collect ammunition returns same to 6 Bty D.A.C.	M.W.
	16.8.17		Nil	
	17.8.17	6 pm	Four Lorries attached for duty to Roads Officer 1st Corps return to sections at E.18.c.0.6 (Map 36B)	M.W.

Vol 36

Confidential.

War Diary
of
No. 2 Cavalry Ammunition Park.

From 1st. Sept. 1914. — To. 30th. Sept. 1914.

Later Became 2 GHQ Reserve M.T. Park

Army Form C. 2118

WAR DIARY
or
INTELLIGENCE SUMMARY
(Erase heading not required.)

Instructions regarding War Diaries and Intelligence Summaries are contained in F.S. Regs., Part II. and the Staff Manual respectively. Title Pages will be prepared in manuscript.

Place	Date	Hour	Summary of Events and Information	Remarks and references to Appendices
GOUY-EN-TERNOIS	1-9-17	7.0 am	Three lorries to S. Blanders for conveyance of troops to the Horse Show.	
"	2-9-17 & 3-9-17		Nothing to report.	
"	4-9-17	2.10 pm	Workshops move to BUNEVILLE. Company ordered there on 5th.	
BUNEVILLE	5-9-17	10.30	Whole of remainder of Park moves to BUNEVILLE.	
"	6-9-17	11.0	J. Baker with Heavy Section (13 pdr) goes on detachment with No 6 A.S.P. just outside BETHUNE.	
"	7-9-17 to 11-9-17		Nothing to report.	
"	12-9-17	7.0 am	Two lorries for fatigue to Seguell.	
"	13-9-17 to 14-9-17		Nothing to report.	
"	15-9-17	7.30 am	Two lorries B.R.E. (3rd F.S.)	
"	16-9-17	9.30 am	Two lorries to O.P.F. for S.A.A. Mills grenades and rounds flares green.	
"	17-9-17 & 18-9-17		Nothing to report.	
"	19-9-17	7.30 am	Two lorries to 2nd F.S.R.E.	
"	20-9-17	10.0 am	Three lorries to O.P.P. for ammunition.	
"	21-9-17 & 27-9-17		Nothing to report — 1 T W G H T goes on leave 22-9-17.	
"	28-9-17	6.30 am	Lorry to BAUPAUME for Pistol Webley ammunition.	
"	29-9-17 & 30-9-17		Nothing to report.	

October 1st 1917.

O.C. 1st A.F.   Forward Major for
O.C. No 2 Cavalry Ammunition Park

Confidential.

War Diary.
of.

No. 2. Cavalry Ammunition Park.

From 1st. Sept. 1914. To. 30th Sept. 1914.

Confidential

War Diary
of
2nd Cav. Divn Ammn Park

From 1st June 1916   To 30th June 1916

WAR DIARY
or
INTELLIGENCE SUMMARY

(Erase heading not required.)

Army Form C. 2118

Place	Date	Hour	Summary of Events and Information	Remarks and references to Appendices
AVROULT	1.6.16	7.30am	Lt Nutel - Orderly Officer. 3 lorries to R.E. for fatigue work.	
"	2.6.16	—	Lt Gallacher - Orderly Officer. — Nothing to report.	
"	3.6.16	7.30am	Lt Nutel - Orderly Officer. Lorry to RE for fatigue work.	
"	4.6.16	—	Lt Gallacher - Orderly Officer. — Nothing to report. — Lt Wright goes on leave.	
"	5.6.16	—	Lt Nutel - Orderly Officer. Lorry to R.E. for fatigue work.	
"	6.6.16	7.30am	Lt Gallacher - Orderly Officer. Two lorries to R.E.	
"	7.6.16	7.30am	Lt Nutel - Orderly Officer. One lorry to R.E. + one to Divisional Signals. Lorry to Sy for collection of grenades etc for practice purposes for Brigades.	
"	8.6.16	9.30am	Lt Gallacher - Orderly Officer. One lorry to 3rd & 5th Brigades with supply of grenades & sandbags & labels of ... S.A.A. for each regiment. — Also one lorry to 2nd A.M. Brigade for same purpose.	
"	9.6.16	—	Lt Nutel - Orderly Officer. Nothing to report.	
"	10.6.16	—	Lt Gallacher - Orderly Officer. Supplied two stretchers to Officer i/c Column 2nd A.C. No 45.	
"	11.6.16	—	Lt Nutel - Orderly Officer. Lt Wright comes off leave.	
"	12.6.16	—	Lt Wright - Orderly Officer. One lorry to DD R.E. — R.54 5 horses reports for duty with the pack. 13th demand returns 121,000 rounds surplus rifles ammunition. (S.A.A.)	

www.ingramcontent.com/pod-product-compliance
Lightning Source LLC
Chambersburg PA
CBHW081430300426
44108CB00016BA/2341